TURNING POINTS

When Everything Changes

Troll Target Series

Troll

TROLL TARGET SERIES

Lewis Gardner	*Senior Editor*
Miriam Rinn	*Editor*
Virginia Pass	*Teaching Guides*
Cris Peterson	*Bibliographies*
Shi Chen	*Cover Illustration*

PROJECT CONSULTANT

David Dillon *Professor of Language Arts, McGill University, Montreal*

ACKNOWLEDGMENTS

"The Treasure of Lemon Brown" reprinted by permission of Miriam Altshuler Literary Agency as agent for Walter Dean Myers. Copyright © 1983 Walter Dean Myers.

"Betrayal" used with permission of the author. Copyright © 1996 Miriam Rinn.

(Acknowledgments continued on page 159)

Printed in the United States of America.   ISBN 0-8167-4275-8

10   9   8   7   6   5   4   3   2   1

C o n t e n t s

The Treasure of Lemon Brown

by Walter Dean Myers

People are not always what they appear to be. Greg doesn't think that a man dressed in rags could own a priceless treasure. But there's a lot that Greg can learn.

The dark sky, filled with angry, swirling clouds, reflected Greg Ridley's mood as he sat on the stoop of his building. His father's voice came to him again, first reading the letter the principal had sent to the house, then lecturing endlessly about his poor efforts in math.

"I had to leave school when I was 13," his father had said, "that's a year younger than you are now. If I'd had half the chances that you have, I'd . . . ."

Greg had sat in the small, pale green kitchen listening, knowing the lecture would end with his father saying he couldn't play ball with the Scorpions. He had asked his father the week before, and his father had said it depended on his next report card. It wasn't often the Scorpions took on new players, especially 14-year-olds, and this was a chance of a lifetime for

Greg. He hadn't been allowed to play high school ball, which he had really wanted to do, but playing for the Community Center team was the next best thing. Report cards were due in a week, and Greg had been hoping for the best. But the principal had ended the suspense early when she sent that letter saying Greg would probably fail math if he didn't spend more time studying.

"And you want to play *basketball?*" His father's brows knitted over deep brown eyes. "That must be some kind of a joke. Now you just get into your room and hit those books."

That had been two nights before. His father's words, like the distant thunder that now echoed through the streets of Harlem, still rumbled softly in his ears.

I t was beginning to cool. Gusts of wind made bits of paper dance between the parked cars. There was a flash of nearby lightning, and soon large drops of rain splashed onto his jeans. He stood to go upstairs, thought of the lecture that probably awaited him if he did anything except shut himself in his room with his math book, and started walking down the street instead. Down the block there was an old tenement that had been abandoned for some months. Some of the guys had held an impromptu checker tournament there the week before, and Greg had noticed that the door, once boarded over, had been slightly ajar.

Pulling his collar up as high as he could, he checked for traffic and made a dash across the street. He reached the house just as another flash of lightning changed the night to day for an instant, then returned the graffiti-scarred building to the grim shadows. He vaulted over the outer stairs and pushed tentatively on the door. It was open, and he let himself in.

The inside of the building was dark except for the dim light that filtered through the dirty windows from the streetlamps. There was a room a few feet from the door, and from where he stood at the entrance, Greg could see a squarish patch of light on the floor. He entered the room, frowning at the musty smell. It was a large room that might have been someone's parlor at one time. Squinting, Greg could see an old table on its side against one wall, what looked like a pile of rags or a torn mattress in the corner, and a couch, with one side broken, in front of the window.

He went to the couch. The side that wasn't broken was comfortable enough, though a little creaky. From this spot he could see the blinking neon sign over the bodega on the corner. He sat a while, watching the sign blink first green then red, allowing his mind to drift to the Scorpions, then to his father. His father had been a postal worker for all Greg's life, and was proud of it, often telling Greg how hard he had worked to pass the test. Greg had heard the story too many times to be interested now.

For a moment Greg thought he heard something that sounded like a scraping against the wall. He listened carefully, but it was gone.

Outside the wind had picked up, sending the rain against the window with a force that shook the glass in its frame. A car passed, its tires hissing over the wet street and its red taillights glowing in the darkness.

Greg thought he heard the noise again. His stomach tightened as he held himself still and listened intently. There weren't any more scraping noises, but he was sure he had heard something in the darkness—something breathing!

He tried to figure out just where the breathing was coming from; he knew it was in the room with him. Slowly he stood, tensing. As he turned, a flash of lightning lit up the room, frightening him with its sudden brilliance. He saw nothing, just the overturned table, the pile of rags, and an old newspaper on the floor. Could he have been imagining the sounds? He continued listening, but heard nothing, and thought that it might have just been rats. Still, he thought, as soon as the rain let up he would leave. He went to the window and was about to look out when he heard a voice behind him.

"Don't try nothin' 'cause I got a razor here sharp enough to cut a week into nine days!"

Greg, except for an involuntary tremor in his knees, stood stock still. The voice was high and brittle, like dry twigs being broken, surely not one he had ever heard before. There was a shuffling sound as the person who had been speaking moved a step closer. Greg turned, holding his breath, his eyes straining to see in the dark room.

The upper part of the figure before him was still in the darkness. The lower half was in the dim rectangle of light that fell unevenly from the window. There were two feet, in cracked, dirty shoes from which rose legs that were wrapped in rags.

"Who are you?" Greg hardly recognized his own voice.

"I'm Lemon Brown," came the answer. "Who're you?"

"Greg Ridley."

"What you doing here?" The figure shuffled forward again, and Greg took a small step backward.

"It's raining," Greg said.

"I can see that," the figure said.

The person who called himself Lemon Brown peered forward and Greg could see him clearly. He was an old man. His black, heavily wrinkled face was surrounded by a halo of crinkly white hair and whiskers that seemed to separate his head from the layers of dirty coats piled on his smallish frame. His pants were bagged to the knees, where they were met with rags that went down to the old shoes. The rags were held on with strings, and there was a rope around his middle. Greg relaxed. He had seen the man before, picking through the trash on the corner and pulling clothes out of a Salvation Army box. There was no sign of the razor that could "cut a week into nine days."

"What are you doing here?" Greg asked.

"This is where I'm staying," Lemon Brown said. "What you here for?"

"Told you it was raining out," Greg said, leaning against the back of the couch until he felt it give slightly.

"Ain't you got no home?"

"I got a home," Greg answered.

"You ain't one of them bad boys looking for my treasure, is you?" Lemon Brown cocked his head to one side and squinted one eye. "Because I told you I got me a razor."

"I'm not looking for your treasure," Greg answered, smiling. "*If* you have one."

"What you mean, *if* I have one," Lemon Brown said. "Every man got a treasure. You don't know that, you must be a fool!"

"Sure," Greg said, as he sat on the sofa and put one leg over the back. "What do you have, gold coins?"

"Don't worry none about what I got," Lemon Brown said. "You know who I am?"

"You told me your name was orange or lemon or something like that."

"Lemon Brown," the old man said, pulling back his shoulders as he did so, "they used to call me Sweet Lemon Brown."

"Sweet Lemon?" Greg asked.

"Yessir. Sweet Lemon Brown. They used to say I sung the blues so sweet that if I sang at a funeral, the dead would commence to rocking with the beat. Used to travel all over Mississippi and as far as Monroe, Louisiana, and east on over to Macon, Georgia. You mean you ain't never heard of Sweet Lemon Brown?"

"Afraid not," Greg said. "What . . . what happened to you?"

"Hard times, boy. Hard times always after a poor man. One day I got tired, sat down to rest a spell, and felt a tap on my shoulder. Hard times caught up with me."

"Sorry about that."

"What you doing here? How come you didn't go on home when the rain come? Rain don't bother you young folks none."

"Just didn't." Greg looked away.

"I used to have a knotty-headed boy just like you." Lemon Brown had half walked, half shuffled back to the corner and sat down against the wall. "Had them big eyes like you got. I used to call them moon eyes. Look into them moon eyes and see anything you want."

"How come you gave up singing the blues?" Greg asked.

"Didn't give it up," Lemon Brown said. "You don't give up the blues; they give you up. After a while you do good for yourself, and it ain't nothing but foolishness singing about how hard you got it. Ain't that right?"

"I guess so."

"What's that noise?" Lemon Brown asked, suddenly sitting upright.

Greg listened, and he heard a noise outside. He looked at Lemon Brown and saw the old man was pointing toward the window.

Greg went to the window and saw three men, neighborhood thugs, on the stoop. One was carrying a length of pipe. Greg looked back toward Lemon Brown, who moved quietly across the room to the window. The old man looked out, then beckoned frantically for Greg to follow him. For a moment Greg couldn't move. Then he found himself following Lemon Brown into the hallway and up darkened stairs. Greg followed as closely as he could. They reached the top of the stairs, and Greg felt Lemon Brown's hand first lying on his shoulder, then probing down his arm until he finally took Greg's hand into his own as they crouched in the darkness.

"They's bad men," Lemon Brown whispered. His breath was warm against Greg's skin.

"Hey! Rag man!" a voice called. "We know you in here. What you got up under them rags? You got any money?"

Silence.

"We don't want to come in and hurt you, old man, but we don't mind if we have to."

Lemon Brown squeezed Greg's hand in his own hard, gnarled fist.

There was a banging downstairs and a light as the men entered. They banged around noisily, calling for the rag man.

"We heard you talking about your treasure." The voice was slurred. "We just want to see it, that's all."

"You sure he's here?" One voice seemed to come from the room with the sofa.

"Yeah, he stays here every night."

"There's another room over there; I'm going to take a look. You got that flashlight?"

"Yeah, here, take the pipe too."

Greg opened his mouth to quiet the sound of his breath as he sucked it in uneasily. A beam of light hit the wall a few feet opposite him, then went out.

"Ain't nobody in that room," a voice said. "You think he gone or something?"

"I don't know," came the answer. "All I know is that I heard him talking about some kind of treasure. You know they found that shopping bag lady with that money in her bags."

"Yeah. You think he's upstairs?"

"HEY OLD MAN, ARE YOU UP THERE?"

Silence.

"Watch my back, I'm going up."

There was a footstep on the stairs, and the beam from the flashlight danced crazily along the peeling wallpaper. Greg held his breath. There was another step and a loud crashing noise as the man banged the pipe against the wooden banister. Greg could feel his temples throb as the man slowly neared them. Greg thought about the pipe, wondering what he would do when the man reached them—what *could* he do.

Then Lemon Brown released his hand and moved toward the top of the stairs. Greg looked around and saw stairs going up to the next floor. He tried waving to Lemon Brown, hoping the old man would see him in the dim light and follow him to the next floor. Maybe, Greg thought, the man wouldn't follow them up there. Suddenly, though, Lemon Brown stood at the top of the stairs, both arms raised high above his head.

"There he is!" a voice cried from below.

11

"Throw down your money, old man, so I won't have to bash your head in!"

Lemon Brown didn't move. Greg felt himself near panic. The steps came closer, and still Lemon Brown didn't move. He was an eerie sight, a bundle of rags standing at the top of the stairs, his shadow on the wall looming over him. Maybe, the thought came to Greg, the scene could be even eerier.

Greg wet his lips, put his hands to his mouth and tried to make a sound. Nothing came out. He swallowed hard, wet his lips once more and howled as evenly as he could.

"What's that?"

As Greg howled, the light moved away from Lemon Brown, but not before Greg saw him hurl his body down the stairs at the men who had come to take his treasure. There was a crashing noise, and then footsteps. A rush of warm air came in as the downstairs door opened, then there was only an ominous silence.

Greg stood on the landing. He listened, and after a while there was another sound on the staircase.

"Mr. Brown?" he called.

"Yeah, it's me," came the answer. "I got their flashlight."

Greg exhaled in relief as Lemon Brown made his way slowly back up the stairs.

"You okay?"

"Few bumps and bruises," Lemon Brown said.

"I think I'd better be going," Greg said, his breath returning to normal. "You'd better leave, too, before they come back."

"They may hang around outside for a while," Lemon Brown said, "but they ain't getting their nerve up to come in here again. Not with crazy old rag men and howling spooks. Best you stay awhile till the coast is clear. I'm heading out west tomorrow, out to East St. Louis."

"They were talking about treasures," Greg said. "You *really* have a treasure?"

"What I tell you? Didn't I tell you every man got a treasure?" Lemon Brown said. "You want to see mine?"

12

"If you want to show it to me." Greg shrugged.

"Let's look out the window first, see what them scoundrels be doing," Lemon Brown said.

They followed the oval beam of the flashlight into one of the rooms and looked out the window. They saw the men who had tried to take the treasure sitting on the curb near the corner. One of them had his pants leg up, looking at his knee.

"You sure you're not hurt?" Greg asked Lemon Brown.

"Nothing that ain't been hurt before," Lemon Brown said. "When you get as old as me, all you say when something hurts is, 'Howdy, Mr. Pain, sees you back again.' Then when Mr. Pain see he can't worry you none, he go on mess with somebody else."

Greg smiled.

"Here, you hold this." Lemon Brown gave Greg the flashlight.

He sat on the floor near Greg and carefully untied the strings that held the rags on his right leg. When he took the rags away, Greg saw a piece of plastic. The old man carefully took off the plastic and unfolded it. He revealed some yellowed newspaper clippings and a battered harmonica.

"There it be," he said, nodding his head. "There it be."

Greg looked at the old man, saw the distant look in his eye, then turned to the clippings. They told of Sweet Lemon Brown, a blues singer and harmonica player who was appearing at different theaters in the South. One of the clippings said he had been the hit of the show, although not the headliner. All of the clippings were reviews of shows Lemon Brown had been in more than 50 years ago. Greg looked at the harmonica. It was dented badly on one side, with the reed holes on one end nearly closed.

"I used to travel around and make money for to feed my wife and Jesse—that's my boy's name. Used to feed them good, too. Then his mama died, and he stayed with his mama's sister. He growed up to be a man, and when the war come he saw fit to go off and fight in it. I didn't have nothing to give him except these things that told him who I was, and what he come from. If you know your pappy did something, you know you can do something too.

"Anyway, he went off to war, and I went off still playing and singing. 'Course by then I wasn't as much as I used to be, not without somebody to make it worth the while. You know what I mean?"

"Yeah," Greg nodded, not quite really knowing.

"I traveled around, and one time I come home, and there was this letter saying Jesse got killed in the war. Broke my heart, it truly did.

"They sent back what he had with him over there, and what it was is this old mouth fiddle and these clippings. Him carrying it around with him like that told me it meant something to him. That was my treasure, and when I give it to him he treated it just like that, a treasure. Ain't that something?"

"Yeah, I guess so," Greg said.

"You *guess* so?" Lemon Brown's voice rose an octave as he started to put his treasure back into the plastic. "Well, you got to guess 'cause you sure don't know nothing. Don't know enough to get home when it's raining."

"I guess . . . I mean, you're right."

"You okay for a youngster," the old man said as he tied the strings around his leg, "better than those scalawags what come here looking for my treasure. That's for sure."

"You really think that treasure of yours was worth fighting for?" Greg asked. "Against a pipe?"

"What else a man got 'cepting what he can pass on to his son, or his daughter, if she be his oldest?" Lemon Brown said. "For a big-headed boy you sure do ask the foolishest questions."

Lemon Brown got up after patting his rags in place and looked out the window again.

"Looks like they're gone. You get on out of here and get yourself home. I'll be watching from the window so you'll be all right."

Lemon Brown went down the stairs behind Greg. When they reached the front door the old man looked out first, saw the street was clear, and told Greg to scoot on home.

"You sure you'll be okay?" Greg asked.

"Now didn't I tell you I was going to East St. Louis in the morning?" Lemon Brown asked. "Don't that sound okay to you?"

"Sure it does," Greg said. "Sure it does. And you take care of that treasure of yours."

"That I'll do," Lemon said, the wrinkles about his eyes suggesting a smile. "That I'll do."

The night had warmed and the rain had stopped, leaving puddles at the curbs. Greg didn't even want to think how late it was. He thought ahead of what his father would say and wondered if he should tell him about Lemon Brown. He thought about it until he reached his stoop, and decided against it. Lemon Brown would be okay, Greg thought, with his memories and his treasure.

Greg pushed the button over the bell marked Ridley, thought of the lecture he knew his father would give him, and smiled.

Betrayal

by Mireille Eckstein

It's not easy to know the right thing to do. For instance, is loyalty more important than the truth? A character in this play comes to a turning point when he must answer that question for himself.

CHARACTERS

JERRY
SHAWN } *young teen-agers*
ANITA

OWNER OF THE CANDY/NEWSPAPER STORE
MRS. BERKOWITZ, *the teacher*

SCENE ONE

JERRY, SHAWN, *and* ANITA, *all wearing backpacks, come into a candy store at once, pushing and laughing loudly. The owner, a man about 50, frowns at them, then goes back to his work behind the counter.*

JERRY [*to* ANITA]: Quit pushing! You almost made me knock those boxes over. [*Takes off his backpack and puts it down. Picks out a comic book from the display.*] Hey, Shawn, look at this—the new *X-Men* comic came in.

> [JERRY *keeps reading the comic book while* SHAWN *drops his backpack on the floor and comes to look over his shoulder.*]

SHAWN: Oh, cool, let me see. What's happening to Fearmaster? Wait, don't turn the page yet, Jerry. I'm not finished.

JERRY: You read too slow. Here, take this one. There's the new issue of *Wrestling Stars*. I'll look at that.

> [JERRY *hands* SHAWN *the comic and picks up a magazine. He and* SHAWN *read, whisper-ing and laughing, while* ANITA *looks at the display rack.*]

STORE OWNER: Hey, what are you doing back there? I've told you before this is a store, not a place to hang out.

JERRY: We're just looking at stuff, sir. We won't mess anything up.

SHAWN [*whispering to* JERRY]: He always says the same thing. What does he think we're doing, having a picnic?

JERRY: Yeah, with his candy. [*Laughs and puts back the magazine.*] Once when I was little, I was here with my mom, and I started to eat some M&M's while she was looking for something. When we got to the register, the owner asked her if she was going to pay for her kid's candy. My mom said, "My son didn't have any candy." So the store guy says, "Then what's in his hand?" Boy, was my mom mad!

SHAWN: Did you get punished? What did she do?

JERRY: I don't remember, so it couldn't have been too bad. I probably couldn't watch TV for a day or something.

> [JERRY *picks up another comic book.*]

SHAWN: My mother would have—[*Pauses, thinking.*] I don't know what, but it would have been worse than that.

JERRY [*Looks at* SHAWN *curiously for a moment, then turns to* ANITA]: Did you find a birthday card for your mother yet, Anita? How about this one? It's funny.

> [JERRY *holds a card out to* ANITA, *who glances at it and*

shakes her head. She holds out a much larger card.]

ANITA: I like this one better.

JERRY: Wow, that's huge. My mother likes the ones with the flowers and glitter, too, but they usually cost a lot. How much is it?

ANITA: I think it's $3.75, but it doesn't matter.

SHAWN: How come? Did you find gold under your bed?

JERRY: Ha! Gold dust, maybe.

ANITA: Because I'm not paying for it, stupid.

[*Kneels down and tucks card in backpack.* JERRY *returns card he's holding to the rack.*]

SHAWN: You can't do that! What if he looks in your bookbag?

ANITA: He's not going to look in my bookbag, stupid. He's going to be busy selling me a candy bar.

JERRY: Yeah, keep him too busy to catch on.

SHAWN [*clearly nervous*]: I don't think—

OWNER: I told you before this is not a library! Get out of there now. [OWNER *walks over to where kids are standing.*] Look what you did to the card rack! I just fixed it. Hey, where is that birthday card that was in the front? The one with the roses.

[JERRY *and* ANITA *pick up their packs and move toward the door.*]

SHAWN [*rushing to return comic book to rack*]: Wait a minute, you guys. I have to get my stuff together.

OWNER: You wait a minute. [*Grabs* SHAWN'S *backpack.*] Let me see what you have in there, you little crook.

SHAWN: Hey, those are all my books. You can't take them!

OWNER: As soon as you came in here, I knew you were trouble. Where are your friends running to? They don't want to get caught, huh? Well, I got you now and I'm not letting you go. Your parents will hear about this!

SHAWN: But I didn't do anything. Please don't call my parents.

OWNER: [*Opens a book, reads the name in the front.*] Shawn Jenkins. [*Looks through books and papers. Puts down the backpack, not having found anything.*] You kids are always in here stealing. I'm sick of it. Get out now, and don't come back.

SCENE TWO

Next day in school. SHAWN, ANITA, *and* JERRY *are sitting at their desks,* SHAWN *behind* ANITA, JERRY *to the side of her. They are working on a social-studies map project.*

JERRY: Hey, Anita, is Shawn talking to you? He won't answer me. I think he's mad about yesterday.

ANITA [*keeps drawing*]**:** Yeah, I guess so.

JERRY: Did he get in trouble?

ANITA: I don't know. If he did, it's his own fault. He should have moved faster.

JERRY: Psst, Shawn. Shawn. What happened at the store? Did the guy yell at you? [SHAWN *keeps his head down and doesn't answer.*] Shawn—

MRS. BERKOWITZ: Is something wrong, Jerry?

JERRY: No, ma'am.

MRS. BERKOWITZ: Well, then, get back to your project, and let Shawn work on his.

JERRY: Yes, ma'am.

> [*Bends to his work for a moment, then looks back at* SHAWN.]

ANITA: Why don't you leave him alone? You're going to get him into more trouble.

> [JERRY *looks at her, then at* SHAWN, *then back at his desk.*]

MRS. BERKOWITZ: All right, class, put away your maps, and then find your partners for your research papers.

> [JERRY *puts away his supplies, then moves his chair over to* SHAWN.]

JERRY [*talking in a low tone*]**:** Tell me now. She'll think we're working.

SHAWN [*looking down at his book*]**:** What do you want me to tell you?

JERRY: You know, what happened after we left. Did he yell? Did he throw you out of the store?

SHAWN [*in a low voice*]**:** He threw me out of the store, then he called my house.

JERRY: What for? You didn't take anything.

SHAWN: He told my mother I was part of a gang that was always shoplifting.

JERRY: A gang! What a liar! Did your mother believe him?

SHAWN: Yes.

JERRY: She did? What did she do?

SHAWN [*hesitates*]: She gave me a beating.

JERRY: For real?

SHAWN [*glances towards teacher, who is looking at them*]: Please don't talk anymore. She's watching us. We have to start working.

> [*Boys bend heads over their books.* ANITA *raises her hand.*]

ANITA: Mrs. Berkowitz, I need help with this part. Could I come up and show it to you, please?

MRS. BERKOWITZ: Certainly, Anita, let me see.

> [ANITA *gets up from her seat, carrying a book, and walks over to* MRS. BERKOWITZ.]

ANITA: I don't know what this word means, off . . . .

MRS. BERKOWITZ: Officious, it means bossy.

ANITA: Thanks, Mrs. Berkowitz, that helps a lot. [*Picks pen off desk.*] Oh, that's a cool pen. It's got four different colors in it.

MRS. BERKOWITZ: A student gave it to me for Christmas last year.

> [ANITA *drops her book, and as she bends down to pick it up, she slips pen into her pocket.*]

ANITA: I'm such a klutz! Well, I better get back to work. Thanks again.

MRS. BERKOWITZ: Any time, Anita. I'm glad to help. [*Fire-drill bell rings as* ANITA *walks back to seat.*] Class, let's put our things away quickly. We'll get back to our map projects after the drill.

SCENE THREE

MRS. BERKOWITZ: All right, everyone, please settle down

now. Take out your maps. We have only a little while left in the period.

JERRY: I'm almost finished anyway. I just have to glue on the labels.

SHAWN: I need some colored pencils. Do you have any colored pencils with points?

JERRY: I don't have any. Ask the teacher.

ANITA: You can use my pen if you want. It has different colors in it. Just be careful.

> [ANITA *hands* SHAWN *the teacher's pen.* SHAWN *takes it and begins to work on his project.*]

JERRY: Where did you get that, Anita? I never saw you use it before.

> [MRS. BERKOWITZ *stands up and begins to look around her desk. Looks on the floor.*]

MRS. BERKOWITZ: Has anyone seen my multicolor pen?

ANITA: I haven't seen it since before, Mrs. Berkowitz. Is it missing?

MRS. BERKOWITZ: Yes, it is, Anita. [*Begins to walk toward student desks, looking around as she goes.*] But I think I've found it now. Shawn, give me my pen, please.

SHAWN: Huh?

MRS. BERKOWITZ: Give me back my pen. There was no need to take it, you know. You could have asked me to lend it to you.

SHAWN: I didn't take it.

MRS. BERKOWITZ: Then how did it get in your hand?

SHAWN: Anita let me use hers.

ANITA: I did not! You're lying! What a liar!

MRS. BERKOWITZ: That's enough. We don't need to discuss this now. Shawn, see me after class, and we'll talk about it then. [*She walks away.*]

JERRY [*whispers*]**:** Anita, you took that pen, didn't you? Now Shawn is going to get into trouble. [ANITA *doesn't look up from her work and doesn't answer.*] That's not fair. You have to tell.

ANITA [*looking over at* JERRY]**:** You must be crazy. Shawn isn't my problem.

JERRY: But he already took the blame for you before!

ANITA [*laughs*]: Then he must be a real loser.

SCENE FOUR

JERRY *is waiting for* SHAWN *outside the classroom.* SHAWN *walks out slowly, closing the door behind him, his head down.*

JERRY: What did she say? Did she believe you?

SHAWN [*Shakes his head. Speaks quietly*]: She's going to call my mother.

JERRY: What will your mother do? [SHAWN *shrugs his shoulders, but doesn't answer.* JERRY *stares at him for a few moments.*] Don't worry, Shawn, she isn't going to call anyone. [JERRY *opens the door and walks back into the classroom.*]

Since Hanna Moved Away

by Judith Viorst

The tires on my bike are flat.
The sky is grouchy gray.
At least it sure feels like that
Since Hanna moved away.

Chocolate ice cream tastes like prunes.
December's come to stay.
They've taken back the Mays and Junes
Since Hanna moved away.

Flowers smell like halibut.
Velvet feels like hay.
Every handsome dog's a mutt
Since Hanna moved away.

Nothing's fun to laugh about.
Nothing's fun to play.
They call me, but I won't come out
Since Hanna moved away.

A Nice Old-Fashioned Romance, with Love Lyrics & Everything

by William Saroyan

The narrator of this story keeps getting in trouble—and sometimes it isn't even his fault! The world of adults turns out to be a difficult place to negotiate, even for the oldest pupil in the fifth grade. In this story set in the early part of this century, what things are different from school life today? What things are the same?

My cousin Arak was a year and a half younger than me, round-faced, dark, and exceptionally elegant in manners. It was no pretense with him. His manners were just naturally that way, just as my manners were bad from the beginning. Where Arak would get around any sort of complication at school with a bland smile that showed his front upper teeth, separated, and melted the heart of stone of our teacher, Miss Daffney, I would go to the core of the complication and with noise and vigor prove that Miss Daffney or somebody else was the culprit, not me, and if need be, I would carry the case to the Supreme Court and prove my innocence.

I usually got sent to the office. In some cases I would get a strapping for debating the case in the office against Mr.

Derringer, our principal, who was no earthly good at debates. The minute I got him cornered he got out his strap.

Arak was different; he didn't care to fight for justice. He wasn't anywhere near as bright as me, but even though he was a year and a half younger than me, he was in the same grade. That wouldn't be so bad if the grade wasn't the fifth. I usually won all my arguments with my teachers, but instead of being glad to get rid of me they refused to promote me, in the hope, I believe, of winning the following semester's arguments and getting even. That's how it happened that I came to be the oldest pupil in the fifth grade.

One day Miss Daffney tried to tell the world I was the author of the poem on the blackboard that said she was in love with Mr. Derringer, and ugly. The author of the poem was my cousin Arak, not me. Any poem I wrote wouldn't be about Miss Daffney, it would be about something worthwhile. Nevertheless, without mentioning any names, but with a ruler in her hand, Miss Daffney stood beside my desk and said, I am going to find out who is responsible for this horrible outrage on the blackboard and see that he is properly punished.

He? I said. How do you know it's a boy and not a girl?

Miss Daffney whacked me on the knuckles of my right hand. I jumped out of my seat and said, You can't go around whacking me on the knuckles. I'll report this.

Sit down, Miss Daffney said.

I did. She had me by the right ear, which was getting out of shape from being grabbed hold of by Miss Daffney and other teachers.

I sat down and quietly, almost inaudibly, said, You'll hear about this.

Hold your tongue, Miss Daffney said, and although I was sore as the devil, I stuck out my tongue and held it, while the little Mexican, Japanese, Armenian, Greek, Italian, Portuguese, and plain American boys and girls in the class, who looked at me for comedy, roared with laughter. Miss Daffney came down on my hand with the ruler, but this time the ruler grazed my

25

nose. This to me was particularly insulting, inasmuch as my nose then, as now, was large. A small nose would not have been grazed, and I took Miss Daffney's whack as a subtle comment on the size of my nose.

I put my bruised hand over my hurt nose and again rose to my feet.

You told me to hold my tongue, I said, insisting that I had done no evil, had merely carried out her instructions, and was therefore innocent, utterly undeserving of the whacked hand and the grazed nose.

You be good now, Miss Daffney said. I won't stand any more of your nonsense. You be good.

I took my hand away from my nose and began to be good. I smiled like a boy bringing her a red apple. My audience roared with laughter and Miss Daffney dropped the ruler, reached for me, and fell over the desk, got up, and began to chase me around the room.

There I go again, I kept saying to myself while Miss Daffney chased me around the room. There I go again getting in a mess like this that's sure to end in murder, while my cousin Arak, who is the guilty one, sits there and smiles. There's no justice anywhere.

When Miss Daffney finally caught me, as I knew she would unless I wanted even more severe punishment from Mr. Derringer, there was a sort of free-for-all during which she tried to gouge my eyes out, pull off my ears, fingers, and arms, and I, by argument, tried to keep her sweet and ladylike.

When she was exhausted, I went back to my seat, and the original crime of the day was taken up again: Who was the author of the love lyric on the blackboard?

Miss Daffney straightened her hair and her clothes, got her breath, demanded and got silence, and after several moments of peace during which the ticking of the clock was heard, she began to speak.

I am going to ask each of you by name if you wrote this awful—poem—on the blackboard and I shall expect you to tell the truth. If you lie, I shall find out anyway and your punishment will be all the worse.

She began to ask each of the boys and girls if they'd written the poem and of course they hadn't. Then she asked my cousin Arak and he also said he hadn't. Then she asked me and I said I hadn't, which was the truth.

You go to the office, she said. You liar.

I didn't write any poem on any blackboard, I said. And I'm not a liar.

Mr. Derringer received me with no delight. Two minutes later Susie Kokomoto arrived from our class with a message describing my crime. In fact, quoting it. Mr. Derringer read the message, made six or seven faces, smiled, snapped his suspenders, coughed and said, What made you write this little poem?

I didn't, I said.

Naturally, he said, you'd say you didn't, but why did you?

I *didn't* write it, I said.

Now don't be headstrong, Mr. Derringer said. That's a rather alarming rumor to be spreading. How do you *know* Miss Daffney's in love with me?

Is she? I said.

Well, Mr. Derringer said, that's what it says here. What gave you that impression? Have you noticed her looking at me with admiration or something?

I haven't noticed her looking at you with anything, I said. Are *you* in love with *her* or something?

That remains to be seen, Mr. Derringer said. It isn't a bad poem, up to a point. Do you really regard Miss Daffney as ugly?

I didn't write the poem, I said. I can prove it. I don't write that way.

You mean your handwriting isn't like the handwriting on the blackboard? Mr. Derringer said.

Yes, I said, and I don't write that kind of poetry either.

You *admit* writing poetry? Mr. Derringer said.

I write poetry, I said, but not *that* kind of poetry.

A rumor like that, Mr. Derringer said. I hope you know what you're about.

Well, I said, all I know is I didn't write it.

Personally, Mr. Derringer said, I think Miss Daffney is not only not ugly, but on the contrary attractive.

Well, that's all right, I said. The only thing I want is not to get into a lot of trouble over something I didn't do.

You *could* have written that poem, Mr. Derringer said.

Not *that* one, I said. I could have written a good one.

What do you mean, *good*? Mr. Derringer said. Beautiful? Or insulting?

I mean beautiful, I said, only it wouldn't be about Miss Daffney.

Up to this point, Mr. Derringer said, I was willing to entertain doubts as to your being the author of the poem, but no longer. I am convinced you wrote it. Therefore I must punish you.

I got up and started to debate.

You give me a strapping for something I didn't do, I said, and you'll hear about it.

So he gave me a strapping and *the whole school* heard about it. I went back to class limping. The poem had been erased. All was well again. The culprit had been duly punished, the poem effaced, and order re-established in the fifth grade. My cousin Arak sat quietly admiring Alice Bovard's brown curls.

First thing during recess I knocked him down and sat on him.

I got a strapping for that, I said, so don't write any more of them.

The next morning, however, there was another love lyric on the blackboard in my cousin Arak's unmistakable hand, and in his unmistakable style, and once again Miss Daffney wanted to weed out the culprit and have him punished. When I came into the room and saw the poem and the lay of the land I immediately began to object. My cousin Arak was going too far. In Armenian I began to swear at him. He, however, had become

28

stone deaf, and Miss Daffney believed my talk was for her. Here, here, she said. Speak in a language everybody can understand if you've got something to say.

All I've got to say is I didn't write that poem, I said. And I didn't write yesterday's either. If I get into any more trouble on account of these poems, somebody's going to hear about it.

Sit down, Miss Daffney said.

After the rollcall, Miss Daffney filled a whole sheet of paper with writing, including the new poem, and ordered me to take the message to the office.

Why *me*? I said. I didn't write the poem.

Do as you're told, Miss Daffney said.

I went to her desk, put out my hand to take the note, Miss Daffney gave it a whack, I jumped back three feet and shouted, I'm not going to be carrying love-letters for you.

This just naturally was the limit. There was a limit to everything. Miss Daffney leaped at me. I in turn was so sore at my cousin Arak that I turned around and jumped on him. He pretended to be very innocent, and offered no resistance. He was very deft, though, and instead of getting the worst of it, he got the least, while I fell all over the floor until Miss Daffney caught up with me. After that it was all her fight. When I got to the office with the message, I had scratches and bruises all over my face and hands, and the love-letter from Miss Daffney to Mr. Derringer was crumbled and in places torn.

What's been keeping you? Mr. Derringer said. Here, let me see that message. What mischief have you been up to now?

He took the message, unfolded it, smoothed it out on his desk, and read it very slowly. He read it three or four times. He was delighted and, as far as I could tell, in love. He turned with a huge smile on his face and was about to reprimand me again for saying that Miss Daffney was ugly.

I didn't write the poem, I said. I didn't write yesterday's either. All I want is a chance to get myself a little education and live and let live.

Now, now, Mr. Derringer said.

He was quite pleased.

If you're in love with her, I said, that's your affair, but leave me out of it.

All I say is you could be a little more gracious about Miss Daffney's appearance, Mr. Derringer said. If she seems plain to you, perhaps she doesn't seem plain to someone else.

I was disgusted. It was just no use.

All right, I said. Tomorrow I'll be gracious.

Now that's better, Mr. Derringer said. Of course I must punish you.

He reached for the lower drawer of his desk where the strap was.

Oh, no, I said. If you punish me, then I won't be gracious.

Well, what about today's poem? Mr. Derringer said. I've got to punish you for that. Tomorrow's will be another story.

No, I said. Nothing doing.

Oh, all right, Mr. Derringer said, but see that you're gracious.

I will, I said. Can I go back now?

Yes, he said. Yes. Let me think this over.

I began to leave the office.

Wait a minute, he said. Everybody'll know something fishy's going on somewhere unless they hear you howl. Better come back here and howl ten times, and then go back.

Howl? I said. I can't howl unless I'm hurt.

Oh, sure you can, Mr. Derringer said. Just give out a big painful howl. You can do it.

I don't think I can, I said.

I'll hit this chair ten times with the strap, Mr. Derringer said, and you howl.

Do you think it'll work? I said.

Of course it'll work, he said. Come on.

Mr. Derringer hit the chair with the strap and I tried to howl the way I had howled yesterday, but it didn't sound real. It sounded fishy, somewhere.

We were going along that way when Miss Daffney herself came into the office, only we didn't know she'd come in, on

30

account of the noise.

On the tenth one I turned to Mr. Derringer and said, That's ten.

Then I saw Miss Daffney. She was aghast and mouth-agape.

Just a few more, son, Mr. Derringer said, for good measure.

Before I could tell him Miss Daffney was in the office, he was whacking the chair again and I was howling.

It was disgusting.

Miss Daffney coughed and Mr. Derringer turned and saw her—his beloved.

Miss Daffney didn't speak. She *couldn't.* Mr. Derringer smiled. He was very embarrassed and began swinging the strap around.

I'm punishing the boy, he said.

I understand, Miss Daffney said.

She didn't either. Not altogether anyway.

I'll not have any pupil of this school being impertinent, Mr. Derringer said.

He was madly in love with her and was swinging the strap around and trying to put over a little personality. Miss Daffney, however, just didn't think very much of punishing the boy by hitting a chair, while the boy howled, the man and the boy together making a mockery of justice and true love. She gave him a very dirty look.

Oh! Mr. Derringer said. You mean about my hitting the chair? We were just rehearsing, weren't we, son?

No, we weren't, I said.

Miss Daffney, infuriated, turned and fled, and Mr. Derringer sat down.

Now look what you've done, he said.

Well, I said, if you're going to have a romance with her, have it, but don't mess me up in it.

Well, Mr. Derringer said, I guess that's that.

He was a very sad man.

All right, he said, go back to your class.

I want you to know I didn't write them poems, I said.

31

That's got nothing to do with it, Mr. Derringer said.

I thought you might want to know, I said.

It's too late now, he said. She'll never admire me any more.

Why don't you write a poem to her yourself? I said.

I can't write poems, Mr. Derringer said.

Well, I said, figure it out some way.

When I went back to class Miss Daffney was very polite. So was I. She knew I knew and she knew if she got funny I'd either ruin the romance or make her marry him, so she was very friendly. In two weeks school closed and when school opened again Miss Daffney didn't show up. Either Mr. Derringer didn't write her a poem, or did and it was no good; or he didn't tell her he loved her, or did and she didn't care; or else he proposed to her and she turned him down, because I knew, and got herself transferred to another school so she could get over her broken heart.

Something like that.

Gift of the Nile

by Jan M. Mike

This tale from ancient Egypt is about 3,500 years old. The rulers of that great civilization were called pharaohs, and they were believed to be gods who had come to earth. Pharaoh Senefru, who appears in this tale, is said to have built the first pyramid.

In the time when Senefru was Pharaoh over all Egypt, a young girl named Mutemwia came to live in the Royal Palace. She was sent by her father as a present to Pharaoh so that she might gain his favor.

Mutemwia soon became a favorite among the women at the palace, for, though she had little beauty, the girl was kind and honest. Pharaoh's magician, Zajamunkhu, upon hearing of her, came to meet her himself. He listened as she played her harp and sang to entertain the other women.

As was his custom, Zajamunkhu ate dinner with Pharaoh Senefru that evening. As they dined, he spoke well of the girl, Mutemwia. Pharaoh had many cares and few people who might share them. So he sent for Mutemwia, that her music might give him rest.

"Long life and health to you, great Pharaoh," Mutemwia said as she entered his room. Her voice was soft and low, and Pharaoh saw that the hand that held her harp trembled.

"Do not fear me, Mutemwia. I would have you play soft music and sing my cares away," Pharaoh said. He reclined upon his couch, and the music of Mutemwia brought him great comfort.

For many nights, Mutemwia came to play for Pharaoh, and soon she lost her fear and grew to care for him greatly. Her music brought them both great joy.

The days passed into weeks. It came to be that Pharaoh spoke to her of his worries and cares, and she listened and gave him good counsel. Each evening, Senefru and Mutemwia talked, until the moon was bright above the Nile.

Senefru learned that Mutemwia was both intelligent and honest. Though many people spoke only to please Pharaoh and said only what they thought he wished to hear, Mutemwia spoke the truth to him always.

One day, word of trouble came from a city in Pharaoh's realm. Senefru had to leave his court and travel for many days. Mutemwia was left to await his return.

When Pharaoh returned, he went to Mutemwia and found her thin and pale. Pharaoh sent for his cooks and ordered them to prepare special foods for Mutemwia.

"You must eat and grow strong, for though you missed me, I have returned," said Senefru, as he fed her with his own hand.

"Long life and health to you, Pharaoh, but I cannot eat. It is true that I missed you, but I also miss my old life. I long for the river I once waded in and the hills I once climbed. This food, to my mouth, tastes like sand, and the air in this room is the air of a tomb. My Pharaoh, I cannot live my life in a cage, however beautiful that cage may be." Mutemwia spoke these words, though she feared they would offend Pharaoh, for they were true words.

Senefru grew angry. His pride was wounded at the thought that Mutemwia missed her freedom more than she had missed him. He drew himself up and left her room without speaking. For many nights after, Pharaoh remained alone.

He did not see Mutemwia. Nor did he give her her freedom, for he feared he would lose her forever if she were allowed to leave. In his private heart he feared he had already lost her.

The days grew hot and sticky. The sun was too bright. Flies buzzed about the palace courtyards. It seemed to Senefru that the people who surrounded him chattered like birds and spoke no more wisdom than the pigs of the farmer. Their games and diversions bored him.

Finally, Pharaoh sent for Zajamunkhu. "My friend," he said to the magician, "food, to my mouth, tastes like sand, and the air in this palace is like the air of a tomb. The people who surround me chatter like birds, and they think of no game to amuse their Pharaoh."

Zajamunkhu was a wise man. He knew of the great friend-ship between Senefru and Mutemwia. Though Pharaoh did not mention her name, Zajamunkhu knew what troubled Pharaoh's heart.

"Peace and long life to you, Pharaoh," he said. "If the air in here is as the air of a tomb, then go forth from the palace. Order a boat to carry you along the cool path of the Nile. Call forth twenty women to row for you. And set one woman above them to steer the boat and sing for you. Then may you see the birds that nest along the river, the green fields, and grassy banks. Then may your heart find contentment."

"You are wise, Zajamunkhu. It shall be as you say."

Zajamunkhu ordered that a boat be brought, and that special oars be made of ebony and electrum. He had new clothes made for each of the women. And he ordered, for each woman, a flower of copper to adorn her hair.

For Mutemwia, who would steer the boat and sing, Pharaoh himself ordered a dress adorned with golden threads. And, for her hair, a golden lotus flower with a heart of blue lapis. These he brought to her when all had been made ready to sail.

Mutemwia gave a cry of joy at seeing Senefru, for she had

missed him. As Pharaoh gave her his gifts, he said, "You cannot leave me, Mutemwia, for you are my most true and honest friend."

Gentle breezes blew over the Nile. The women who rowed the boat were strong and graceful. Mutemwia's voice was sweet to Pharaoh's ears as she steered the boat and sang.

Pharaoh saw the birds that nested along the Nile, the green fields, and the grassy banks. He saw Mutemwia's cheeks grow rosy in the warmth of the sun, and his heart was content.

So he might have remained, but a harsh wind rose up and took from Mutemwia's hair the golden lotus that Pharaoh had given her. Mutemwia stopped singing and cried out in dismay as she watched her flower sink beneath the surface of the Nile. Without her song to guide them, the women could not row, and the boat was stilled.

"Do not cry, Mutemwia. Only sing and steer the boat, and I will give you a hundred golden flowers when we return," Senefru called to her.

"Long life and health to you, Pharaoh. I do not want a hundred flowers, only the one that you gave me this day, when you told me I was your most true and honest friend."

Zajamunkhu saw that the women had ceased to row, and he grew concerned. He approached Pharaoh, and Senefru told him what had happened.

"Peace and long life to you, Pharaoh," said Zajamunkhu. "I will do what I can, and in truth it is no great magic to me."

Zajamunkhu spoke words of power, and the air grew thick with silence as the mighty Nile split down the middle, like a stone of granite under the tools of a mason. He lifted his staff, and lightning flashed forth from it, and, lo, half of the river rose into the air and lay itself atop the other half.

Pharaoh's boat drifted slowly through the air and came to rest on the dry river bed. Beside the boat the river loomed, so high it seemed to touch the very sky. Everyone was frightened to see the wall of water, held fast by nothing more than the magician's words. Even Pharaoh looked upon the wall of water in great wonderment and forgot all else.

Only one person paid no attention to the water. Mutemwia was neither frightened nor astonished. Along the dry river bed, she saw a flash of gold in the summer light. Swiftly, she climbed out of the boat and ran to get her golden lotus. Grasping it in her hand, she returned to the boat.

Zajamunkhu brought down his staff and spoke more words of power. Slowly, the boat rose in the air, and the water returned to its proper place. Once more, Pharaoh's boat rested upon the tranquil Nile.

Mutemwia turned to Senefru, and he saw that the love she held for him was true. Such friendship was a gift of the heart and needed no cage to hold it.

"This golden lotus, that you rescued, will forever be my pledge of love to you," said Pharaoh to Mutemwia. "I can see the friendship you hold for me. Therefore, I will give you your freedom and a house near the palace, and in this way we will be friends for many years."

So it came to be that Mutemwia left the Royal Palace and lived in her own house. Many people came to her for counsel and advice, and she prospered and grew rich as the years passed. To the end of her days she wore no other jewelry than the golden lotus of Senefru. And always she remained the most true and honest friend to Pharaoh.

The Open Window

by Peter St. Croix

Based on a Story by Saki

Are those figures coming across the lawn, toward the open window, ghosts? A stranger in town can be made to feel welcome—or he can learn about terrifying things that happen in quiet places. Vera tells Mr. Nuttel more about her family than is good for his nerves. Saki is the pen name of H.H. Munro, a Scottish writer famed for his imaginative and humorous short stories. He was killed in France during World War I.

CHARACTERS

VERA, *15 years old*

FRAMTON NUTTEL

MRS. SAPPLETON, *Vera's aunt*

MR. SAPPLETON, *who may be a ghost*

RONNY, *Mrs. Sappleton's brother, who also may be a ghost*

> *A living room with a large window overlooking a terrace. The window, which can be used as a door, is now open. It is the late afternoon, beginning to get dark.* FRAMTON NUTTEL, *a very nervous man, is speaking with* VERA.

VERA: My aunt will be down in a minute, Mr. Nuttel. Until then, you'll have to put up with me.

FRAMTON: Oh, please. You're fine. I mean—I'm just fine, and you—well, you're a perfectly fine substitute. I mean, don't worry. I mean, I'm not worried. My doctor said I mustn't worry so much.

VERA: Have a chocolate?

FRAMTON: No. I mean, thank you. No, thank you. In fact, that's why I'm here. In Mountain Ridge, I mean. My doctor said I should get away from everything and rest, and so I came to Mountain Ridge for a vacation.

VERA: Oh, I'm sure you'll find Mountain Ridge restful. There's absolutely nothing to do. How do you happen to know my aunt?

FRAMTON: I don't. I mean, I don't know your aunt at all. I don't know anybody.

VERA: You don't?

FRAMTON: No, I don't. But my sister was afraid when I came here, I would just stay by myself and not speak to anyone. So she gave me the names of people she knows. She stayed here once, so she knows lots of people. It was four years ago. She stayed at the same bed-and-breakfast I'm staying at, the Blue Mongoose.

VERA: So you don't know anyone around here?

FRAMTON: Oh, no. Your aunt was the first person I had the courage to call. I guess her name sounded nice—"Mrs. Sappleton" sounded like a nice name.

VERA: Then you know nothing about my aunt? No one's told you anything?

FRAMTON: No—I only called her, and she asked me to visit. She told me how to walk here from the Blue Mongoose. You go through the little park . . . .

VERA: Yes, I know. My aunt's great tragedy happened just three years ago, so of course your sister couldn't know about it.

FRAMTON: Her tragedy? What kind of tragedy could happen in a quiet place like Mountain Ridge?

VERA: You may have wondered why we keep that window

wide open on an October afternoon.

FRAMTON: Well, it's quite warm for this time of year. Don't you think so? Oh, dear—does that window have something to do with the tragedy?

VERA: Out through that window, exactly three years ago, her husband and her younger brother went off for a day of hunting. They never came back. In crossing the dark swamp to their favorite rabbit-hunting place, they were engulfed in quicksand. It had been that dreadful wet summer, you know, and places that were safe in other years gave way suddenly without warning. Their bodies were never recovered. That was the dreadful part of it.

FRAMTON [*very upset*]: Oh, my word. How terribly, terribly awful.

VERA: My poor aunt always thinks they'll come back some day, they and the little brown spaniel that was lost with them. She expects them to walk in through that window just as they used to do. That's why the window is kept open every evening till it is quite dark. Poor Aunt, she's often told me how they went out, her husband with his tan raincoat over his arm, and Ronny, her youngest brother, singing "The Hunter Woke in the Morning," as he always used to do. He did it to tease her, because she said it got on her nerves. [*She offers him another chocolate, which he refuses. She starts eating one of the chocolates.*] Do you know, sometimes on still, quiet evenings like this, I almost get a creepy feeling that they will walk in through that window . . . .

[*She shudders.* FRAMTON *is extremely nervous.*]

FRAMTON: Oh, dear. I can understand how scary that—oh, yes, I can understand. Oh!!

[*He jumps as* MRS. SAPPLETON *enters the room.*]

MRS. SAPPLETON: Mr. Nuttel—Mr. Nuttel—you must accept my apologies for neglecting you like this! You'd be surprised how busy life can be in a quiet little town like Mountain Ridge. I thought I'd never get off the phone with Laura Thorne—we're planning a fundraiser for the garden club.

FRAMTON: Oh, no, I'm . . . .

MRS. SAPPLETON: I hope Vera has been amusing you?

FRAMTON: Yes, she's been very interesting.

VERA: I've given him some of the local history.

MRS. SAPPLETON: Have you? I hope you don't mind the open window, Mr. Nuttel. My husband and my brother will be home soon from a day of hunting, and they always come in this way. [FRAMTON *and* VERA *exchange a worried look.*] They've gone after rabbits near the swamp, so they'll make a fine mess on my poor carpets. Men are like that, I suppose.

FRAMTON [*trying to make conversation*]: Oh, let's be fair— I've known women who are not terribly neat.

MRS. SAPPLETON: Have you? Especially when they go hunting, I suppose?

FRAMTON [*eager to change the subject*]: Tell me about the garden club fundraiser.

MRS. SAPPLETON: Oh, no, you would find it terribly boring. If you're interested in hunting, though, my husband could tell you about the best places to try. He's such a fanatic—my brother, also—going out whenever they can spare the time. Squirrels, rabbits, raccoons—tramping all over that swamp, till it gets dark.

FRAMTON: As a matter of fact, I've been ordered, by my doctors, to get as much rest as possible and to avoid all kinds of excitement. Because of my nerves. I often suffer spells of nervous exhaustion.

MRS. SAPPLETON: I don't see why a little hunting wouldn't be relaxing. We'll have to ask my husband about it. [*Looking outside*] Oh, good! Here they are! Just look at them—don't they look as if they were muddy up to the eyes!

> [FRAMTON *stands up. He sees that* VERA *is looking outside in horror.*]

FRAMTON: Oh, my word. Is that—? Who are those men? It's so dark—can you recognize them? They have guns—and a small dog—and one of them is carrying a raincoat . . . . [*He is terrified.*]

RONNY [*offstage, singing*]:

The hunter woke in the morning

And found his head was not in view.

"Mother dear," he said, "I need my head

And my trusty .22!"

> [*During the song,* FRAMTON *has screamed and fled from the room.*]

MRS. SAPPLETON: Where is he going?

VERA [*looking toward the front of the house*]: Out of the house! He knocked over your Chinese vase, but it isn't broken.

MRS. SAPPLETON: What a terribly odd person.

> [MR. SAPPLETON *and* RONNY *enter through the open window.*]

MR. SAPPLETON: Here we are, my dear. Fairly muddy, but most of it's dry now. Who was that who ran out as we got to the terrace?

MRS. SAPPLETON: A strange man, a Mr. Nuttel. He kept talking about his nerves, and then he dashed off without a word of goodbye or apology when you arrived. You'd think he had seen a ghost!

VERA: I think it was the dog.

MR. SAPPLETON: The dog? Why?

VERA: He told me he had a horror of dogs. He was once chased into a cemetery by a pack of wild dogs. He had to spend the night in a newly dug grave with the creatures snarling and foaming just above him. Enough to make anyone lose their nerve.

RONNY: Vera, that sounds suspiciously like one of *your* stories.

VERA: Oh, no. Mr. Nuttel told me every word of it. That's why he's so nervous. He also told me about the time they operated on him and he died on the operating table and then—

MRS. SAPPLETON: You can tell us at dinner. You can also tell us what you did to poor Mr. Nuttel, to scare him so badly. Now, run along with Ronny. You can help him skin the rabbits.

Ozymandias

by Percy Bysshe Shelley

I met a traveler from an antique land
Who said: Two vast and trunkless legs of stone
Stand in the desert . . . Near them, on the sand,
Half sunk, a shattered visage lies, whose frown,
And wrinkled lip, and sneer of cold command,
Tell that its sculptor well those passions read
Which yet survive, stamped on these lifeless things,
The hand that mocked them, and the heart that fed:
And on the pedestal these words appear:
"My name is Ozymandias, king of kings:
Look on my works, ye Mighty, and despair!"
Nothing beside remains. Round the decay
Of that colossal wreck, boundless and bare
The lone and level sands stretch far away.

On the Vanity of Earthly Greatness

by Arthur Guiterman

The tusks that clashed in mighty brawls
Of mastodons, are billiard balls.

The sword of Charlemagne the Just
Is ferric oxide, known as rust.

The grizzly bear whose potent hug
Was feared by all, is now a rug.

Great Caesar's bust is on the shelf,
And I don't feel so well myself.

A Mother in Mannville

by Marjorie Kinnan Rawlings

*All good stories include turning points. Sometimes the
action starts moving in a different direction. Sometimes
a character's—or the reader's—understanding changes.
Where is the turning point in this story of a lonely boy
and the woman who befriends him?*

The orphanage is high in the Carolina mountains.
Sometimes in winter the snowdrifts are so deep that the
institution is cut off from the village below, from all the
world. Fog hides the mountain peaks, the snow swirls down the
valleys, and a wind blows so bitterly that the orphanage boys
who take the milk twice daily to the baby cottage reach the
door with fingers stiff in an agony of numbness.

"Or when we carry trays from the cookhouse for the ones
that are sick," Jerry said, "we get our faces frostbit, because we
can't put our hands over them. I have gloves," he added. "Some
of the boys don't have any."

He liked the late spring, he said. The rhododendron was in
bloom, a carpet of color across the mountainsides, soft as the
May winds that stirred the hemlocks. He called it laurel.

"It's pretty when the laurel blooms," he said. "Some of it's pink and some of it's white."

I was there in the autumn. I wanted quiet, isolation, to do some troublesome writing. I wanted mountain air to blow out the malaria from too long a time in the subtropics. I was homesick, too, for the flaming of maples in October, and for corn shocks and pumpkins and black-walnut trees and the lift of hills. I found them all, living in a cabin that belonged to the orphanage, half a mile beyond the orphanage farm. When I took the cabin, I asked for a boy or man to come and chop wood for the fireplace. The first few days were warm, I found what wood I needed about the cabin, no one came, and I forgot the order.

I looked up from my typewriter one late afternoon, a little startled. A boy stood at the door, and my pointer dog, my companion, was at his side and had not barked to warn me. The boy was probably twelve years old, but undersized. He wore overalls and a torn shirt, and was barefooted.

He said, "I can chop some wood today."

I said, "But I have a boy coming from the orphanage."

"I'm the boy."

"You? But you're small."

"Size don't matter, chopping wood," he said. "Some of the big boys don't chop good. I've been chopping wood at the orphanage a long time."

I visualized mangled and inadequate branches for my fires. I was well into my work and not inclined to conversation. I was a little blunt.

"Very well. There's the ax. Go ahead and see what you can do."

I went back to work, closing the door. At first the sound of the boy dragging brush annoyed me. Then he began to chop. The blows were rhythmic and steady, and shortly I had forgotten him, the sound no more of an interruption than a consistent rain. I suppose an hour and a half passed, for when I stopped and stretched, and heard the boy's steps on the cabin stoop, the sun was dropping behind the farthest mountain, and

46

the valleys were purple with something deeper than the asters.

The boy said, "I have to go to supper now. I can come again tomorrow evening."

I said, "I'll pay you now for what you've done," thinking I should probably have to insist on an older boy. "Ten cents an hour?"

"Anything is all right."

We went together back of the cabin. An astonishing amount of solid wood had been cut. There were cherry logs and heavy roots of rhododendron, and blocks from the waste pine and oak left from the building of the cabin.

"But you've done as much as a man," I said. "This is a splendid pile."

I looked at him, actually, for the first time. His hair was the color of the corn shocks and his eyes, very direct, were like the mountain sky when rain is pending—gray, with a shadowing of that miraculous blue. As I spoke, a light came over him, as though the setting sun had touched him with the same suffused glory with which it touched the mountains. I gave him a quarter.

"You may come tomorrow," I said, "and thank you very much."

He looked at me, and at the coin, and seemed to want to speak, but could not, and turned away.

"I'll split kindling tomorrow," he said over his thin ragged shoulder. "You'll need kindling and medium wood and logs and backlogs."

At daylight I was half wakened by the sound of chopping. Again it was so even in texture that I went back to sleep. When I left my bed in the cool morning, the boy had come and gone, and a stack of kindling was neat against the cabin wall. He came again after school in the afternoon and worked until time to return to the orphanage. His name was Jerry; he was twelve years old, and he had been at the orphanage since he was four. I could picture him at four, with the same grave gray-blue eyes and the same—independence? No, the word that comes to me is "integrity."

The word means something very special to me, and the quality for which I use it is a rare one. My father had it—there is another of whom I am almost sure—but almost no man of my acquaintance possesses it with the clarity, the purity, the simplicity of a mountain stream. But the boy Jerry had it. It is bedded on courage, but it is more than brave. It is honest, but it is more than honesty. The ax handle broke one day. Jerry said the woodshop at the orphanage would repair it. I brought money to pay for the job and he refused it.

"I'll pay for it," he said. "I broke it. I brought the ax down careless."

"But no one hits accurately every time," I told him. "The fault was in the wood of the handle. I'll see the man from whom I bought it."

It was only then that he would take the money. He was standing back of his own carelessness. He was a free-will agent and he chose to do careful work, and if he failed, he took the responsibility without subterfuge.

And he did for me the unnecessary thing, the gracious thing, that we find done only by the great of heart. Things no training can teach, for they are done on the instant, with no predicated experience. He found a cubbyhole beside the fire-place that I had not noticed. There, of his own accord, he put kindling and "medium" wood, so that I might always have dry fire material ready in case of sudden wet weather. A stone was loose in the rough walk to the cabin. He dug a deeper hole and steadied it, although he came, himself, by a short cut over the bank. I found that when I tried to return his thoughtfulness with such things as candy and apples, he was wordless. "Thank you" was, perhaps, an expression for which he had no use, for his courtesy was instinctive. He only looked at the gift and at me, and a curtain lifted, so that I saw deep into the clear well of his eyes, and gratitude was there, and affection, soft over the firm granite of his character.

He made simple excuses to come and sit with me. I could no more have turned him away than if he had been physically hungry. I suggested once that the best time for us to visit was just before supper, when I left off my writing. After that, he waited always until my typewriter had been some time quiet. One day I worked until nearly dark. I went outside the cabin, having forgotten him. I saw him going up over the hill in the twilight toward the orphanage. When I sat down on my stoop, a place was warm from his body where he had been sitting.

He became intimate, of course, with my pointer, Pat. There is a strange communion between a boy and a dog. Perhaps they possess the same singleness of spirit, the same kind of wisdom. It is difficult to explain, but it exists. When I went across the state for a weekend, I left the dog in Jerry's charge. I gave him the dog whistle and the key to the cabin, and left sufficient food. He was to come two or three times a day and let out the dog, and feed and exercise him. I should return Sunday night, and Jerry would take out the dog for the last time Sunday afternoon and then leave the key under an agreed hiding place.

My return was belated and fog filled the mountain passes so treacherously that I dared not drive at night. The fog held the next morning, and it was Monday noon before I reached the cabin. The dog had been fed and cared for that morning. Jerry came early in the afternoon, anxious.

"The superintendent said nobody would drive in the fog," he said. "I came just before bedtime last night and you hadn't come. So I brought Pat some of my breakfast this morning. I wouldn't have let anything happen to him."

"I was sure of that. I didn't worry."

"When I heard about the fog, I thought you'd know."

He was needed for work at the orphanage and he had to return at once. I gave him a dollar in payment, and he looked at it and went away. But that night he came in the darkness and knocked at the door.

"Come in, Jerry," I said, "if you're allowed to be away this late."

"I told maybe a story," he said. "I told them I thought you would want to see me."

"That's true," I assured him, and I saw his relief. "I want to hear about how you managed with the dog."

He sat by the fire with me, with no other light, and told me of their two days together. The dog lay close to him, and found a comfort there that I did not have for him. And it seemed to me that being with my dog, and caring for him, had brought the boy and me, too, together, so that he felt that he belonged to me as well as to the animal.

"He stayed right with me," he told me, "except when he ran in the laurel. He likes the laurel. I took him up over the hill and we both ran fast. There was a place where the grass was high and I lay down in it and hid. I could hear Pat hunting for me. He found my trail and he barked. When he found me, he acted crazy, and he ran around and around me, in circles."

We watched the flames.

"That's an apple log," he said. "It burns the prettiest of any wood."

We were very close.

He was suddenly impelled to speak of things he had not spoken of before, nor had I cared to ask him.

"You look a little bit like my mother," he said. "Especially in the dark, by the fire."

"But you were only four, Jerry, when you came here. You have remembered how she looked, all these years?"

"My mother lives in Mannville," he said.

For a moment, finding that he had a mother shocked me as greatly as anything in my life has ever done, and I did not know why it disturbed me. Then I understood my distress. I was filled with a passionate resentment that any woman should go away and leave her son. A fresh anger added itself. A son like this one— The orphanage was a wholesome place, the executives were kind, good people, the food was more than adequate, the boys were healthy, a ragged shirt was no hardship, nor the doing of clean labor. Granted, perhaps, that the boy felt no lack, what blood fed the bowels of a woman who did not yearn over this child's lean body that had come in parturition out of her own? At four he would have looked the same as now. Nothing, I thought, nothing in life could change those eyes. His quality must be apparent to an idiot, a fool. I burned with questions I could not ask. In any, I was afraid, there would be pain.

"Have you seen her, Jerry—lately?"

"I see her every summer. She sends for me."

I wanted to cry out, "Why are you not with her? How can she let you go away again?"

He said, "She comes up here from Mannville whenever she can. She doesn't have a job now."

His face shone in the firelight.

"She wanted to give me a puppy, but they can't let any one boy keep a puppy. You remember the suit I had on last Sunday?" He was plainly proud. "She sent me that for Christmas. The Christmas before that"—he drew a long breath, savoring the memory—"she sent me a pair of skates."

"Roller skates?"

My mind was busy, making pictures of her, trying to understand her. She had not, then, entirely deserted or forgotten him. But why, then—I thought, "I must not condemn her without knowing."

"Roller skates. I let the other boys use them. They're always borrowing them. But they're careful of them."

What circumstance other than poverty—

"I'm going to take the dollar you gave me for taking care of Pat," he said, "and buy her a pair of gloves."

I could only say, "That will be nice. Do you know her size?"

"I think it's 8½," he said.

He looked at my hands.

"Do you wear 8½?" he asked.

"No. I wear a smaller size, a 6."

"Oh! Then I guess her hands are bigger than yours."

I hated her. Poverty or no, there was other food than bread, and the soul could starve as quickly as the body. He was taking his dollar to buy gloves for her big stupid hands, and she lived away from him, in Mannville, and contented herself with sending him skates.

"She likes white gloves," he said. "Do you think I can get them for a dollar?"

"I think so," I said.

I decided that I should not leave the mountains without seeing her and knowing for myself why she had done this thing.

T he human mind scatters its interests as though made of thistledown, and every wind stirs and moves it. I finished my work. It did not please me, and I gave my thoughts to another field. I should need some Mexican material.

I made arrangements to close my Florida place. Mexico immediately, and doing the writing there, if conditions were favorable. Then, Alaska with my brother. After that, heaven knew what or where.

I did not take time to go to Mannville to see Jerry's mother, nor even to talk with the orphanage officials about her. I was a trifle abstracted about the boy, because of my work and plans. And after my first fury at her—we did not speak of her again—his having a mother, any sort at all, not far away, in Mannville, relieved me of the ache I had had about him. He did not question the anomalous relation. He was not lonely. It was none of my concern.

He came every day and cut my wood and did small helpful favors and stayed to talk. The days had become cold, and often I let him come inside the cabin. He would lie on the floor in front of the fire, with one arm across the pointer, and they would both doze and wait quietly for me. Other days they ran with a common ecstasy through the laurel, and since the asters were now gone, he brought me back vermilion maple leaves, and chestnut boughs dripping with imperial yellow. I was ready to go.

I said to him, "You have been my good friend, Jerry. I shall often think of you and miss you. Pat will miss you too. I am leaving tomorrow."

He did not answer. When he went away, I remember that a new moon hung over the mountains, and I watched him go in silence up the hill. I expected him the next day, but he did not come. The details of packing my personal belongings, loading my car, arranging the bed over the seat, where the dog would ride, occupied me until late in the day. I closed the cabin and started the car, noticing that the sun was in the west and I should do well to be out of the mountains by nightfall. I stopped by the orphanage and left the cabin key and money for my light bill with Miss Clark.

"And will you call Jerry for me to say good-by to him?"

"I don't know where he is," she said. "I'm afraid he's not well. He didn't eat his dinner this noon. One of the other boys saw him going over the hill into the laurel. He was supposed to fire the boiler this afternoon. It's not like him; he's unusually reliable."

I was almost relieved, for I knew I should never see him again, and it would be easier not to say good-by to him.

I said, "I wanted to talk with you about his mother—why he's here—but I'm in more of a hurry than I expected to be. It's out of the question for me to see her now too. But here's some money I'd like to leave with you to buy things for him at Christmas and on his birthday. It will be better than for me to try to send him things. I could so easily duplicate—skates, for instance."

She blinked her honest spinster's eyes.

"There's not much use for skates here," she said.

Her stupidity annoyed me.

"What I mean," I said, "is that I don't want to duplicate things his mother sends him. I might have chosen skates if I didn't know she had already given them to him."

She stared at me.

"I don't understand," she said. "He has no mother. He has no skates."

The Day the Batboy Played

by Bruce Nash & Allan Zullo

In the space of a moment, your fondest wish can come true. This is the true account of the day a Georgia minor-league team was losing 13-0, and a batboy joined the pros.

Twelve-year-old Joe Reliford lived the dream of every Little Leaguer, every sandlot ballplayer, every kid who loves baseball. Joe pinch-hit and played the outfield in a professional baseball game—and set a record as the youngest pro ballplayer in the history of the national pastime.

In 1952, Joe was the batboy for the Fitzgerald Pioneers, a minor-league team in the Class D Georgia State League. He was a good-natured, eager-to-please youngster whom the players liked. In fact, the Pioneers often let Joe practice with them before games. He would shag fly balls and sneak into the batting cage where he'd take a few swings. Even though he was only 4 feet, 11 inches tall and weighed just 70 pounds, Joe could really hit the ball.

His favorite player was speedy second baseman Charlie

Ridgeway, who often sat with the batboy on the team bus, talking baseball as they rode from town to town. In July, the president and manager of the Pioneers appointed Ridgeway to manage the team during road games.

Ridgeway had been the manager for a week when the Pioneers traveled to Statesboro to play the Pilots in a sold-out night game on July 19. To the joy of the fans, the Pilots began clobbering the Pioneers. By the eighth inning, Statesboro was slaughtering Fitzgerald 13–0.

Suddenly, a fan shouted to Ridgeway, "Hey, why don't you put in the batboy! Your players ain't doin' diddly!" Another fan chimed in, "Yeah, put in the batboy!" Soon the entire grandstand was chanting, "Put in the batboy! Put in the batboy!"

Ridgeway looked at Joe, who was beginning to feel nervous, and figured that since the game was a lost cause anyway, why not make a little history? So Ridgeway called time and talked with the umpire, Ed Kubick. "They're hollering for the batboy, Eddie," the manager said. "He's got a uniform and he can hit the ball. Is there anything in the rules that says I can't play him?"

"He's not eligible to play," said the ump. "But I don't see any harm in it. Just understand that if you win, you'll have to forfeit."

"That's not likely to happen," replied Ridgeway. He then went back to the dugout and told the batboy, "Joe, grab a bat and pinch-hit for [Ray] Nitchting."

Joe's mouth dropped open in shock. His stomach started turning somersaults and his knees began to shake. "You're not serious, are you?" stammered Joe. "I'm just a batboy."

"Well, they're hollerin' for a batboy, so we'll give 'em a batboy," Ridgeway said. "Now, go get a stick and go up there."

Joe was so stunned he could barely move. Somehow he mustered the strength to find a bat and walk up to the plate as the crowd howled with glee. Statesboro pitcher Curtis White shook his head in disbelief and asked the umpire if it was okay to pitch to the youngster. The umpire nodded yes.

The fans were on their feet, laughing and shouting at Joe.

"C'mon, kid, hit it out of the park!" "Show those big bums on your team how to hit the ball!" "Let's see you club one!" "Don't be scared!"

But Joe was scared. He took some healthy practice swings and some deep breaths to calm his nerves. Then Joe got ready for the first pitch.

White, who was working on a two-hit shutout, wasn't about to go easy on the youngster. The hurler's first pitch to Joe was a fastball that blazed across the plate for a called strike. White cut loose with another fastball that sailed past Joe before he could even think about taking the bat off his shoulder. "Strike two!" shouted the umpire. The crowd booed the call and urged Joe to hang in there.

Joe stepped out of the batter's box and told himself to expect a fastball. He settled back in and waited for the next pitch. Sure enough, it was another fastball. But this time, Joe was ready and he smashed the ball hard down the third-base line. The crowd rose to its feet, thinking he might get a double. But the third baseman made a great play by spearing the ball and throwing to first to get Joe out by a step. Even though he had grounded out, Joe received a standing ovation.

He received another big cheer when Ridgeway sent him to right field in the bottom of the eighth. Leadoff hitter Charlie Quimby then belted a pitch down the right-field line for an easy stand-up double. But Quimby decided to test Joe's arm, so he scampered toward third. Joe cleanly scooped up the ball and fired a perfect strike to the cutoff man, who nailed Quimby at third. Again, the crowd cheered for Joe.

But the youngster made an even more stunning play moments later. Batter Jim Schuster clubbed a deep fly that sent Joe dashing back as far as he could go. Then Joe jumped up, timing his leap perfectly. He caught the ball just before it would have sailed over the fence. Joe had just robbed Schuster of a home run!

The fans were so excited that they streamed out of the grandstand and onto the field where they shook Joe's hand and pounded his back. Even Schuster offered his congratulations. Others showed their appreciation by stuffing nickels, dimes, and quarters into Joe's pocket.

Although the Pioneers had lost 13–0, Joe was so happy he couldn't wipe the grin off his face for hours. In the clubhouse, one of the Pioneers told Ridgeway, "You better sign him to a contract, Skipper, before he gets away." Even though Joe never played in a real game again, he was forever proud of his one moment of fame. As Ridgeway told his team after the game, "Boys, you've just been part of history. Our team has the youngest player ever to play in a professional baseball game."

The Nauga Hunters

by Matthew Cheney

The unknown can be the most frightening force of all.
The boys in this story must find the strength to deal
with the future, no matter what it holds. The author
wrote this story when he was an eighth-grade student
in New Hampshire.

Hank, a 13-year-old boy with wispy brown hair and spindly legs, spotted his little brother sitting on the floor of the living room, watching a cartoon.

"Hey, Chucky, wanna go nauga hunting?" asked Hank.

"What's a nauga?" asked Chucky, turning away from the television.

"A nauga's a little thing—'bout the size of a cat—that has big long teeth and a red feather for a tail," explained Hank, with the appropriate hand movements.

"A featha for a tail?"

"Yup. And naugas can change color so we can't see 'em, 'cept for the tail; that don't change color."

"How we gonna hunt the naugas then, if we don't see nothin' but the tail?"

"Well, we'll hafta look all over the woods, and if we see a red tail movin', then we'll shoot it."

"I don't wanna shoot it."

"Aw, come on, Chucky, ya gotta shoot naugas."

"Why can't we jus' keep 'im for a pet?"

"'Cause naugas eat people."

"Oh. What if he got to like me?"

"Naugas don't like nobody."

"Nobody?"

"Nobody. So, you gonna come nauga hunting with me or not?"

"You sure they don't like nobody? I mean, the Tylers' dog likes me, and he don't like nobody."

"Naugas don't like nobody. Period. Now, I'll give you five seconds to make up your mind. One. Two. Three—"

"Nobody?"

"Come on, Chucky! I told you they don't like nobody. Now, you comin' or not?"

"I'll come."

"Good. Now, let's go up to my room and get the water guns."

Hank filled his black Colt water gun in the bathtub while Chucky filled his bright green Luger in the sink. They pressed the white plastic plugs into the filling holes and stuck the guns into the holsters that were attached to their belts.

Hank put his camouflage army cap onto his head. "I wanna cap!" came Chucky's high-pitched scream.

"I don't have another."

"Then I'll go get Dad's."

"It won't fit."

"My butt it won't."

"Okay. Don't say I didn't tell ya, 'cause I did tell ya." Chucky waddled down the stairs and Hank followed shortly. He was carrying an old backpack that had been sitting in his closet since the beginning of time.

Chucky was downstairs in the den closet. Hank couldn't see his little brother in the shadows of the closet, but every now and then a coat or a hat or a boot would fly out and land on the floor amidst a pile of other coats, hats, and boots.

"Chucky! Whatcha cleanin' out the closet for?!"

"Gotta find a hat."

"Dad's is right here. What's wrong with Dad's? Thought that was the one you wanted."

"Don't fit."

"I told ja so. Come on, the naugas'll be hibernatin' soon."

Chucky climbed over a pile of coats that lay before him and stood looking at Hank. "Ain't got a hat."

"Chucky, will you come on! I try to be nice to you for once and whatta you do? You just say, 'I ain't got a hat,' like I really care. Here, take mine." Hank angrily took off his cap and hit Chucky in the chest with it. Chucky took it. "Now pick up these clothes and let's get goin' already!"

The sky was clear of clouds and birds. It was a blue that can only be seen on brisk autumn days, a Pacific blue. The air was vivacious, the trees lit with the color of their leaves, the hills a massive fruit salad.

"I don't see no naugas," said Chucky.

"You won't for a little while. We ain't deep 'nough inta the woods yet."

Chucky crackled along behind his brother.

"Will you stop stepping on all the leaves! You'll scare the naugas away."

"Didn't mean to."

"I don't care if you meant to or not, just be quiet. Some hunter you are."

They plodded together through the woods like a pair of senile tigers. Then Hank stopped and held up his left hand. He pulled his Colt out of its holster. "Nauga," he whispered.

"Where?"

He pointed to a wet, rotting log that lay across a small trench.

"In there?" asked Chucky.

"Yup. Now, he don't know we've seen him, so be wicked quiet and walk up there, onto the hill, just so you're looking over the hole. I'm gonna try ta flush 'im out."

"You sure I gotta go there alone?"

"Wimp."

"Okay, I'll go. *Sheesh*."

Hank snuck forward, very quietly, and peeked under the log. He heard his little brother walking above him. "There it goes!" screamed Hank. "Shoot it!" He looked up as Chucky squirted water in all directions. Then he brought up his plastic Colt and squirted Chucky.

"Hey!" exclaimed Chucky, the thin blasts of water still hitting him. Hank lowered his gun. "Whatcha do that for?"

"You're stupid. You really believed in naugas? Prob'ly believe in dragons and Santa Claus, too."

"Huh? What's wrong 'bout Santa?"

"Ain't no such thing! No Santa and no naugas, stupid!"

"Then why'd ja take me out here then?"

"I dunno."

"C'mon, Hank. Why? We got all dressed up an' stuff an' then there ain't no naugas? Why?"

"It ain't important."

"You jus' wanted ta trick me, that's all. Jus' wanted me ta look stupid."

"No. No, that weren't it."

"Come on then, tell me." He waited for a moment, but Hank made no move to answer. "I'll tell Mom. I'll tell her you tricked me and took me out here jus' ta get me wet. I'll tell her you threw me in the brook. I'll tell her you jus' wanted me ta get peenamonia." Hank walked away from Chucky and sat on a damp rock. "I'm goin' home," said Chucky.

"Then go on."

"Hank, why'd ja take me out here? C'mon, I won't tell nobody."

Silence. Chucky again: "Is it about Sally?"

"No, 'course not."

"I betcha broke up with her and you jus' wanted ta take it out on me."

"I woulda beaten you up then."

"Is it about school? You mad 'cause you got a bad grade or somethin'?"

"No. I'm use ta bad grades. Listen, jus' go home. I'll be back in a while."

Chucky stood next to his brother without saying anything. Then he asked quietly, "Is it about Mom and Dad?"

"Jus' beat it!"

"What's gonna happen? Is Dad gonna leave?"

"You wanna know? You really wanna know, you little jerk? Las' night I heard Mom and Dad talkin'."

"Fightin'?"

"Nope, jus' talkin'. Dad said he's gonna leave and go ta New York and take me, and Mom can have you. So I brought you out here jus' ta be nice 'cause I may never really be able ta do anythin' like this again. Okay? Satisfied?"

"You sure yer tellin' the truth?"

Hank stood up and jumped on his brother; they fell to the damp ground. His eyes were sparkling and his lips were unfirm. "Would I lie about that, you little . . . " His voice faded as he pulled his arm up to punch Chucky. Chucky was crying now. Hank stood up. "Forget it," he said. "Supper'll be almost ready." Chucky was still on the ground. "You comin'?"

Chucky pulled himself up and brushed off his rear end. His face was streaked with tears. "Yup," he said softly.

"Well, hurry up. Then after supper maybe we can go hunt some more naugas. They ain't invisible at night."

"Thought you said they ain't real—like dragons."

"You believed me? Boy, maybe you *are* stupider than you look." He turned around and headed for home, his little brother trying to keep up.

Superman: The Neglected Parents

by Nathan Aaseng

Superman revolutionized the comic-book business. The cartoonists who created the Man of Steel, however, did not benefit from the phenomenal success of their superhero.

Superman, the legendary defender of truth, justice, and the American way, was originally designed as a symbol for everything that was good about the United States. Some of the shine was rubbed off his bright blue tights and red cape in an article published in 1975 in the *New York Times,* however. Given the "justice" dealt Superman's creators, the comic strip character could also be seen as a symbol of corporate power.

Superman originated not on the planet Krypton, but in Cleveland, Ohio. The year was 1932, and the United States was in the middle of the paralyzing Great Depression. But the bleak economic environment did not daunt the spirits of two 17-year-old Cleveland high school students. Jerry Siegel was determined to forge a career as a writer, and his friend Joe Shuster wanted to make his mark in the field of art. Both young men fed their imaginations by reading science fiction magazines. Impatient to get on with their careers, they began to create stories and publish them in their own magazine, which they called *Science Fiction.*

Siegel wrote one story about an evil scientist. "Reign of the Superman" was inspired by the acrobatic feats of one of his favorite movie actors, Douglas Fairbanks, Jr. It is hard to imagine now, but in the 1930s, "super" was not a common part of people's vocabulary. Siegel chose the name Superman because it sounded authoritative. Shuster added illustrations and the story appeared in the boys' *Science Fiction* magazine in 1933. The two began toying with the idea of making a comic strip out of it.

Neither had a clear idea of how to do that until the summer of 1934. Kept awake one night by a muggy July heat wave, Siegel let his thoughts wander. He thought of ways to improve the Superman character. By morning, he had so fleshed out his new character that he was ready for Shuster to begin drawing immediately. The new Superman was a heroic, almost invincible character, fighting to preserve the ideals of the United States. In a time of hardship for most Americans, Siegel hoped the character might boost people's spirits.

His ideas borrowed heavily from much science fiction of the time, particularly a novel entitled *Gladiator* by Philip Wylie. Siegel decided that his character would be dressed in a colorful, tight-fighting costume. Born on another planet, he would come to earth and become a powerful defender of freedom and justice. He would maintain his privacy by living a normal life as an ordinary person, revealing his secret identity to no one.

After Shuster had completed the artwork, the two tried to sell their comic strip. Most news syndicates turned them down altogether. A few expressed interest but called for changes that Siegel and Shuster were unwilling to make.

Frustrated about their future to sell the Superman concept, the two boys turned to other comic book stories to earn a living. They sold two features, "Slam Bradley" and "Spy," to a comic book publisher named Harry Donenfield. In 1938 Donenfield was looking for material for a comic series he was starting called *Action Comics.* He asked the advice of M. C. Gaines, who was considered one of the top authorities on comic books. Gaines recommended Siegel and Shuster's Superman.

After more than four years of discouragement, the two young men had found a buyer. In June, 1938, the Superman comic strip first appeared on newsstands. The response was overwhelming. Before long Superman was the most popular comic character in the country. Superman radio and television series were started, followed by cartoon shows and movies. Not only did Superman ensure the success of *Action Comics,* but it provided a boost for the entire comic book industry. Leagues of superheroes followed Superman to enchant youngsters for generations.

Since publishers and producers have made millions of dollars from the Superman character, one would think that Siegel and Shuster became millionaires at a young age. But they were too inexperienced to know what rights they had and how to protect them. The men sold the rights to the character of Superman to their employer for a small amount of money. For a few years, they produced all the work on the Superman strip for *Action Comics* for about $15 per page. After a few years, however, Shuster's eyesight began to fail, and the two young men were replaced by other, more polished artists.

Siegel and Shuster sued to gain control of their creation and to receive a share of the enormous profits that others were reaping. Although they earned some money from Superman products, they didn't win back the rights they had naively sold.

While Superman enjoyed celebrity status, his two creators fell into poverty. Shuster's eyesight was so poor that he could get only low-paying manual jobs. Legally blind, he lived in a threadbare New York City apartment. Nearly 40 years after he had drawn the first pictures of Superman for the world, he had to depend on a brother to help him pay his bills. At the same time, 61-year-old Jerry Siegel was working as a poorly paid clerk for the state of California. Although he had continued to write for D.C. Comics (owner of *Action Comics*) until the late 1960s, his financial situation had become so desperate that he had once sold his precious collection of old comic books to make some money.

Over the years, the two men had fought for a share of the Superman profits. At last they admitted defeat and, in 1975, they turned to newspapers to publicize the injustice of their situation. Shortly after a news conference they held—at which they were supported by cartoonists throughout the country—they obtained a settlement. The owners of the Superman rights agreed to pay each of the creators of Superman a pension for the rest of their lives.

While the money offered desperately needed comfort to the two men, it was still just a tiny percentage of what others had made from Superman, and it was more than 30 years late in coming. Superman had gone on to fame and fortune. But he left his parents behind.

Thanksgiving Day

by Julia Remine Piggin

Based on a Story by O. Henry

Some of O. Henry's best-known stories turn on incidents of miscommunication. There's something Stuffy Pete doesn't know about Henry Vanderhyden—and Stuffy Pete's secret could land him in the hospital!

CHARACTERS

JEFFERSON SMITH
STUFFY PETE } *New York City street people*
HENRY VANDERHYDEN, *70, member of an old New York family*
WAITER ONE
WAITER TWO
WOMAN PASSERBY
MAN IN CROWD
WOMAN IN CROWD
DR. MARCH
STRETCHER BEARER
DR. LAKE
DR. MELLON

NURSE ANGELI
NURSE FILENE

NON-SPEAKING

PEOPLE IN CROWD
STRETCHER BEARER TWO
ORDERLY ONE
ORDERLY TWO

SCENE ONE

[*Union Square Park, New York City, Thanksgiving Day, 1899. The park is deserted and the benches are empty, under gray skies threatening snow.*
[JEFFERSON SMITH *and* STUFFY PETE *enter. They stagger to a bench and sprawl on it, unbuttoning their ragged jackets and shirts.*]

JEFFERSON: What a spread! Thank you, Pilgrims, for coming over here and making this day possible.

STUFFY: Yeah, it was sure some dinner.

JEFFERSON: Just think, Stuffy. If we had been five minutes earlier or even a minute later when we passed that house on Washington Square, somebody else would have had that feed!

STUFFY: That's right, Jefferson.

JEFFERSON: When that man in that fancy uniform stepped out of that gate and tapped me on the shoulder, I thought I was in trouble. I thought, "Jefferson Smith, you better start running!" And then he said [JEFFERSON *tries to imitate a British accent.*] "Sir, if you are not engaged for dinner, would you join Miss Edna and Miss Caroline Livingston? They send me to invite a stranger every year, and I am sure your friend would be welcome also." Hah! [*He laughs, slapping his knee.*] If I wasn't so full I can hardly breathe, I'd still think it was a dream. Whew!

STUFFY: I felt like running, too. Probably should have.

JEFFERSON: What? Stuffy, friend, are you out of your mind? Oysters. Turkey and baked potatoes. Hot biscuits, dripping with butter. Chicken salad. Squash pie. Plum pudding. All the ice cream in the world. Every year those women bring in a stranger or two. There have been times when I thought I hated rich people from old New York families, thinkin' they're better than I am, but today—bless 'em. I don't think I'll ever be able to eat again.

STUFFY: I will. I have to eat another dinner in half an hour.

JEFFERSON: What? Friend, that brandy sauce on the pie must have gone right to your head. Where would you eat another dinner, even if you could manage to get it down, which you couldn't?

STUFFY [*pointing to the distance*]: Look over there. What do you see?

JEFFERSON [*shielding his eyes with his hand*]: Somebody walkin' this way. Can't make out much till they come closer.

STUFFY: It's another rich old family. Henry Vanderhyden. Whatever kind of books they get their names printed in, he's in.

JEFFERSON: So? What's Henry Sandy-hye, or whatever you said his name is, got to do with us?

STUFFY: With me. He's coming for me.

JEFFERSON: Friend, you *did* eat too much. You don't make any sense at all. Why would this man be coming for you?

STUFFY [*groaning*]: More philanthropy. I've met him at this bench for nine years on Thanksgiving Day. First time, I was really down and out—planning to raid a few garbage cans to keep my ribs from rattling. This gentleman came across Fourth Avenue, just as he will in a minute. He took me to a restaurant and bought me a Thanksgiving dinner. When he left me, he said, "I'll see you next year at the same place, sir, at which we so fortunately met today." That's the way he talks. I didn't believe him. But just for the heck of it, I showed up here the next Thanksgiving. And so did he. Today'll be the 10th time.

JEFFERSON: Send a bird with a feather to knock me down with!

STUFFY: I found out a few things about him over all these

69

dinners. Lives in some rooms he rents in one of those old brownstones over to the east. Got a little greenhouse the size of a trunk and raises some kind of flowers. That's in the winter. In the spring he walks in the Easter parade. In the summer he goes to some old farmhouse out in New Jersey, and sits on the porch in an armchair. Hopes someday to find some kind of fancy butterfly. Ornitho—oh, well, a butterfly.

JEFFERSON: What about his family? He got one?

STUFFY: I dunno. I sort of think he might wish he had a son. He looks at me kind of sad sometimes, as if he wondered what I'd be like if I was somebody else. But what I am is Thanksgiving. I'm a tradition. Kind of an institution. Something that has to be done, or you feel funny. Like the flowers and New Jersey and the butterfly. You know, you salute the flag, and think about George Washington when you tell a lie.

JEFFERSON: You're beginning to lose me, friend. Anyway, why don't you just get up before he gets here, and beat it out of the park? You can't eat another dinner, he won't find you, and that'll be that. If he asks me, I'll tell him I don't know anybody who looks like you. And think about George Washington, of course.

STUFFY: No, I can't do that.

JEFFERSON: Come on, pal, why not?

STUFFY: I just can't. It's just—I can't. I'm Thanksgiving. It's the way it is. A tradition. I'm it. There's something special about that. Sacred, like.

JEFFERSON: Well, I don't want to stay to see it. If you burst, it'll be real messy. See you around here tomorrow, if you're still alive. Here he comes. Hey, right out of the past. Old-fashioned suit and cane.

STUFFY [as HENRY VANDERHYDEN *enters and walks toward the bench*]: He looks a lot thinner and older. Stick around, Jeff, and listen. He always says the same thing.

JEFFERSON: Me, too, at times like this: goodbye.

> [*He walks away, as* HENRY VANDERHYDEN *comes up to the bench.*]

70

HENRY: Good morning. I am glad to perceive that the vicissitudes of another year have spared you to move in health about the beautiful world. For that blessing alone, this day of thanksgiving is well proclaimed to each of us. If you will come with me, my man, I will provide you with a dinner that should make your body as joyful as your mind.

> [STUFFY *looks at* HENRY VANDERHYDEN, *helplessly, and makes a strangled sound.* HENRY *smiles brightly.* STUFFY *manages to speak.*]

STUFFY: Thank you, sir. I'll go with you. I'm—much obliged.

HENRY: I hope you're hungry.

STUFFY [*gulping*]: Famished.

> [HENRY *gestures toward the exit from the park, and they go out together.*]

SCENE TWO

> *A restaurant.* STUFFY PETE *and* HENRY VANDERHYDEN *sit at a table.* HENRY *is beaming as* STUFFY *manfully attacks a piece of pie, eating slowly but determinedly. Two* WAITERS *stand a short distance away, watching them.*

WAITER ONE: Happens every year, you say?

WAITER TWO: Yup, regular as a grandfather's clock. Old man brings in the bum, watches while the bum puts away enough food to give the Grand Old Army indigestion. Y'know, I think he's about stuffed to the gills. Look how red his face is.

> [*At the table,* STUFFY *leans back in his chair.*]

STUFFY: Thank you, sir, thank you, that was a wonderful meal.

> [*He stands, his eyes glazing, and stumbles in the direction of the kitchen.*]

WAITER ONE [*grabbing his arm*]: Here sir, you're going the wrong way. You're heading for the kitchen. The door's in that direction.

> [*He turns* STUFFY *around and points him toward the door.* HENRY VANDERHYDEN *is counting out the price of the dinner, hesitates, and then leaves a tip for the*

71

waiter. He catches up with STUFFY, *and they go out the door together. In the street,* HENRY *pauses.*]

HENRY: Well, sir, another Thanksgiving has almost passed. Another blessed, satisfying day in the most honorable tradition of this city and ourselves. Next year—[*He breaks off, his face somber.*]

STUFFY [*almost unable to speak*]: Oh, yes, sir, I—

HENRY: My pleasure. We walk in opposite ways, I believe.

> [*He turns and exits toward the east.* STUFFY *takes a few steps in the opposite direction, totters, seems to sway in the wind, and falls heavily to the sidewalk.*]

WOMAN PASSERBY: Hey, what's the matter? Mister, are you all right? [*A crowd begins to gather.*]

MAN IN CROWD: Send for an ambulance!

WOMAN IN CROWD: Drunk. That's how they give thanks—they get drunk. Disgusting.

DR. MARCH [*pushing his way through the crowd to* STUFFY'S *side.*]: I'm a doctor—let me through, please. [*He kneels beside* STUFFY *and smells his breath.*] He's not drunk. There's no odor of liquor at all. It's something else—I don't know what. Is that ambulance on the way?

> [*Two men in white coats, carrying a stretcher, run in, push through the crowd.*]

STRETCHER BEARER ONE: Here we are. Stand back, let's get him on the stretcher.

DR. MARCH: Get him to the hospital as soon as you can.

STRETCHER BEARER ONE: We're trying, Doc. [*They roll* STUFFY *onto the stretcher and lift it.*] Wow, he's heavy as a lead elephant. Stand back, folks! Happy Thanksgiving! [*They exit with* STUFFY.]

WOMAN IN CROWD [*as it begins to disperse*]: If he's not drunk, I'm Queen Victoria.

SCENE THREE

Later on Thanksgiving afternoon. A ward in a New

York City hospital. STUFFY PETE *lies on a bed, surrounded by* DR. LAKE, DR. MELLON, DR. MARCH, NURSE ANGELI, *and* NURSE FILENE.

DR. LAKE: He's not drunk. Not a whiff of liquor on his breath.

DR. MARCH: I know. The people who saw it happen said he just seemed to puff out the rags he had on, like an owl puffs out its feathers. Then he fell to the sidewalk like a horse with sunstroke.

DR. LAKE: Very descriptive. But why?

DR. MELLON: Have there been any reports of epidemics in the tropics? Maybe he's a sailor, and he picked up some disease on a voyage.

DR. MARCH: Sailors don't have to dress in rags like his. And I don't see any tattoos on his skin.

DR. LAKE: Skin. The skin on his abdomen is stretched so tight, a child could play a game of jacks on it. It looks as if he'd swallowed a cannonball.

DR. MELLON: The ambulance crew who brought him in said he weighed enough to be full of lead.

[*He pokes at* STUFFY'S *abdomen.* STUFFY *groans.*]

DR. LAKE: I'd like to see what's in there. Nurse Angeli, can you find out if the operating room is available?

NURSE ANGELI [*smiling sweetly*]: Yes, Doctor, right away.

DR. LAKE [*fondly*]: Hurry back. [NURSE ANGELI *exits.*]

NURSE FILENE: Should I draw some more blood, Doctor?

DR. MELLON: We've already drawn enough blood from him to soak a battlefield.

[STUFFY *moans, moves, tries to speak but can't.*]

DR. MARCH: Hey, there, fellow! [*Leans over* STUFFY, *shouts into his ear.*] How do you feel? Are you in pain? What happened?

[STUFFY *tries to speak again, but only makes strangled sounds.*]

DR. LAKE: That's all right, my friend. If you can't tell us, we'll find out anyway.

STUFFY [*choking it out*]: Ate. Ate, ate.

NURSE FILENE: Eight. What does he mean by eight?

DR. LAKE: I don't know. Eight o'clock? Something happened at eight o'clock?

DR. MARCH: What comes in eights? Pieces of eight! That's what pirates are always burying on desert islands.

DR. MELLON: I told you he was a sailor.

DR. LAKE: Doctor, he can't be a pirate. Where's his cutlass? He's just an ordinary New York street bum.

> [STUFFY *moans again, speaks, but his speech is hard to understand.*]

STUFFY: Tradition. Had to. Nine times.

DR. LAKE: There you are. He's had this condition nine times.

NURSE FILENE: Then why did he say eight?

DR. LAKE: He lost count. Doctors, we've got to find out about that cannonball.

> [*While the last few speeches are spoken, two orderlies have brought another patient on a stretcher and lifted him onto a bed farther down the ward. As they work,* NURSE ANGELI *enters, walks past them, stops, looks at the patient, and walks on to* STUFFY'*s bed.*]

NURSE ANGELI: The operating room is free, Doctor.

DR. LAKE: Very good work, Nurse Angeli. Are we all agreed, gentlemen? [*Murmurs of assent.*] Very well. Orderly! Orderly! What are they taking so long about down there?

NURSE ANGELI: Oh, Doctor, it's so odd. That patient is another man who fell in the street. Only he didn't swell up. Far from it.

DR. LAKE: How far from it?

NURSE ANGELI: Dr. Willing admitted him and they talked. His name is Henry Vanderhyden. He's from one of the oldest families in New York.

DR. LAKE: You don't say? Well, what happened? Did his blue blood boil over?

NURSE ANGELI: Doctor! It's really very sad.

DR. LAKE [*holding out a square of cloth*]: My handkerchief.

NURSE ANGELI: He told Dr. Willing that he had come down in the world. All he has left is his honor. Doctor saw he was close to starvation—he hasn't had anything to eat in three days.

The One Who Watches

by Judith Ortiz Cofer

Doris really likes her friend Yolanda, but she can't do the things that Yolanda does. Yolanda is heading for trouble, Doris's mother warns. Will Doris follow her there?

Mira! Mira!" my friend Yolanda yells out. She's always telling me to look at something. And I always do. I look, she does. That's the way it's always been. Yolanda just turned sixteen, I'm six months younger. I was born to follow the leader, that's what my mother says when she sees us together, and it's true.

It's like the world is a deli full of pricey treats to Yolanda, and she wants the most expensive ones in fancy boxes, the ones she can't afford. We spend hours shopping downtown. Sometimes when Yolanda gets excited about an outfit, we go into the store and she tries it on. But the salespeople are getting to know us. They know we don't have any money. So we get chased out of places a lot. Yolanda always yells at the security man, "I've been thrown out of better places than this!" And we have.

One time Yolanda and I skipped school and took a bus into the city—just because Yolanda wanted to look around the big store on Thirty-fourth Street. They were having a teen fashion show that day, for all the rich girls in New York and their overdressed mothers. And guess what? Yolanda sneaked into one of the dressing rooms, with me following her, and she actually got in line for one of the dresses being handed out by all these busy-looking women with tape measures around their necks who called all the girls "honey" and measured their chest, waist, and hips in about thirty seconds flat. Then this guy in a purple skintight body suit screeches out, "Hey, you!" and I nearly pass out, thinking we had gotten caught.

"Those earrings are monstrous!" he screams at Yolanda, who's wearing pink rubber fish earrings to match her pink-and-black striped minidress.

"Here, try these!" He hands her a set of gold hoops in a very fancy black velvet box; then he screams at another model. I go into a dressing stall to hide and Yolanda runs in and sits on my lap, laughing her head off.

"Mira, Doris, mira." She shows me the earrings, which look like real gold. I hug Yolanda—I just love this girl. She's crazy and will try anything for fun.

I help Yolanda put on the dress she says she's going to model. The price tag inside says $350.00. It's my turn to say "Mira" to Yolanda. She shrugs.

"I ain't gonna steal it, Doris," she says. "I'm just gonna walk down that runway, like this." She walks out of the dressing room with one hand on a hip, looking like a real model in a green velvet dress, gold earrings, and her white sneakers. The man in the body suit runs up to her, screaming, "No, no! What do you think you're doing? Those shoes are monstrous!" He waves over one of the women with measuring tapes around their necks and has her take down Yolanda's shoe size. Soon I'm helping her try on shoes from a stack as tall as I am. She decides on black patent leather pumps.

There's such confusion back there that Yolanda doesn't get

caught until the girls are lined up for the show to begin. Then nobody can find Yolanda on the list. She really does a good job of acting offended at all the trouble. I think it's her New Jersey Puerto Rican accent that gives her away. The others talk with their noses way up in the air, sounding like they have a little congestion.

"Whaddaya mean my name ain't there?" Yolanda demands, sticking her nose up there in orbit too.

I just stand to the side and watch everything, pretending that it's a play and Yolanda is the star. I promise myself that if it gets too dangerous, I'll just slip out. See, I'm not flashy like Yolanda. I'm practically invisible. My hair is kinky, so I keep it greased down, and I'm short and plain. Not ugly, not beautiful. Just a nothing. If it wasn't for Yolanda, nobody would know I'm around. She's great, but she scares me, like the modeling thing at the store. I have enough problems without getting arrested. So I tell myself that if the police come, I'll just make myself invisible and walk away. Then I'd be really alone. If Yolanda knew how scared I really am, she'd leave me anyway. Yolanda always says that nothing scares her except scary people. She says she hates a snitch worse than anything, and that's what scared people do, she tells me. They blame others for their troubles. That's why she dumped her last best friend, Connie Colón. Connie got scared when her mother found out she'd been skipping school with Yolanda, and told. Yolanda gets a cold look in her eyes when she talks about Connie, like she wants her dead. I don't want Yolanda to ever look at me that way.

Anyway, a big bossy woman came to lead us to her office on the top floor. It was bigger than my bedroom and her desk was at least the size of my bed. There was a rug under our feet that was as thick as a fur coat. From her window you could see most of New York. She looked at Yolanda with an expression on her face like I see on people walking by street people. It's like they want to ask them, "What are you doing on *my* sidewalk?" The lady didn't even look at me, so I glued myself to the gray wall.

"Young lady, do you realize that what you did today could

be considered a crime?" She spoke very slowly, sounding out each word. I guess she knew by now that we were Puerto Rican and wanted to make sure we understood.

Yolanda didn't answer. They had made her take off the velvet dress, the shoes, and the earrings. The woman who carried them out with her fingertips put them in a plastic bag before handing them to this woman in front of us now.

Holding up the plastic bag in front of Yolanda, she asked another question: "Do you know how much money the things you took are worth?"

I watched Yolanda get up slowly from tying her shoe-strings. She put on her pink fish earrings next without any hurry. Then she straightened out her tight skirt. She still looked offended. And maybe like she wanted a fight.

"I wasn't stealing your *theengs*," she said, imitating the woman's uptown accent.

"Then what were you doing in our dressing room, trying to disrupt the fashion show?"

"No. I was going to model the dress." Yolanda put her hands on her hips as if daring the woman to argue with her.

"Model? You wanted to model clothes *here*?" The woman laughed. "Young lady—"

"My name is Yolanda." Yolanda was getting angry, I could tell by the way she made her eyes flash at the woman, like a cat getting ready to pounce. It was strange to watch Yolanda, who is barely five feet tall, facing off with this big woman in a gray suit and high heels.

"All right, Yolanda. Let me tell you something. You can't just decide to be a model, sneak into a dressing room, and go on a runway. These girls have been to modeling school. They have been practicing for weeks. Did you really think you could get away with this?" She was sounding angry now. I edged toward the door. "I'll tell you what. I'm not going to turn you in. I'm going to have our security guard escort you outside. And I never want to see you in this store again. Look." She pointed to a camera practically invisible on the ceiling.

78

"We have pictures of you now, Yolanda." She finally looked over at me. "And of your partner there. If you come back, all I have to do is show them to the judge."

We were shown the way out to Thirty-fourth Street by the security guard, who looked just like any rich shopper in his wool sweater and expensive jeans. You never know who's watching you.

So Yolanda is telling the truth when she tells the store people that we've been thrown out of better places. She's always looking for a better place to get thrown out of. But the Thirty-fourth Street store may be hard to beat.

That same day we went up to the eighty-sixth floor of the Empire State Building—it's just down the street from the store. Yolanda went all around the viewing deck like a child, yelling out, "Mira! Mira!" from every corner. She was feeling good.

At home there is always salsa music playing, but it's not because anyone is happy or feels like dancing. To my parents music is a job. They're both in a Latino music band called ¡Caliente! He plays the drums and she sings, so they're always listening to tapes. They play at the same barrio club every night, the Caribbean Moon, and the regular customers want to hear new songs every week. So Mami sings along with the tapes, but she looks bored while she's doing it. Most of my life she stopped singing only to tell me to do something or to yell at me. My father doesn't say much. He's hardly ever around during the day; either he sleeps until the afternoon, since they play sets until three in the morning, or he goes down to the basement to practice his drums. The super of our building, Tito, is his best friend and lets Papi keep his drums in a storage room near the washers and dryers. Our apartment has walls thin and crumbly as old cardboard, and if he tried to play drums in it they'd probably crash around our heads.

My mother is singing along with Celia Cruz, the old Cuban *salsera*, when I come in. She's at the stove, sautéing some codfish. I can smell the olive oil simmering, but I'm not hungry.

Yolanda and I ate a whole bagful of butterscotch candy. She wouldn't tell me where she got it and I never saw her buy it, although I spent the whole day with her.

"*Hola*, Doris, how's school?" my mother asks. But she doesn't look at me and she doesn't wait for me to answer. She just keeps on singing something about leaving the cold American city and going home to a lover in the sun. I stand there watching her; I'm feeling invisible again. The tape ends and she asks me where I've been, since school let out hours ago.

"New York."

She finally looks at me and smiles as if she doesn't believe me. "I bet you've been following that Yolanda around again. Niña, I'm telling you that señorita is trouble. She's trying to grow up too fast, sabes? Mira. . . ." Mami takes my chin into her hand that smells like oregano and garlic and other Island spices. She looks really tired. She's short like me and we look a lot alike, but I don't think she's noticed. "Doris, tonight is not a school night, why don't you come to the club with us and listen to some music?" She's asked me to do that once a week for years, but I'm not interested in hanging out at a cheap night-club with a bunch of drunks. Besides, I'd have to sit in the back the whole time because I'm a minor. In case the police do a check—I can slip out the kitchen door. When I was little, I had to go with them a lot, and it wasn't fun. I'd rather stay home by myself.

I shake my head and go into my room. I put a pillow over my face so I won't hear the music and my mother singing about people in love and islands with beaches and sun.

I spend all day Saturday at Yolanda's. We have the place to ourselves because her mother works weekends. She believes in spiritism, so there are candles everywhere with things written on the glass jars like "For money and luck," and "For protection against your enemies," and "To bring your loved one home." She's got a little table set up as an altar with statues of *santos* and the Virgin Mary, and a picture of her dead husband, Yolanda's father, who was killed during a robbery. Yolanda says she doesn't remember him that well anymore, even though it's only a couple of years since he died.

The place is stuffy with incense smells, and Yolanda tells me we are going shopping today.

"You got money?" I notice that she's wearing a big raincoat of her mother's. It's made of shiny bright green plastic and it has huge pockets. I start feeling a little sick to my stomach and almost tell her I'm going home to bed.

"I got what it takes, honey." Yolanda models the ugly rain-coat for me by turning around and around in the small room.

We have to pass my apartment on our way out, and I can hear my mother singing an old song without the usual music tape accompanying her in the background. I stop to listen. It's "Cielito Lindo"—a sort of lullaby that she used to sing to me when I was little. Her voice sounds sweet, like she is really into the song for once. Yolanda is standing in front of me with her hands on her hips, giving me a funny look like she thinks I'm a sentimental baby. Before she says something sarcastic, I run down the stairs.

Yolanda is not just window-shopping today. She tells me that she's seen something she really wants. When we get to the store—one of the most expensive ones downtown—she shows me. It's a black beaded evening bag with a long strap. She puts it on over her shoulder.

"It's cute," I tell her, feeling sicker by the minute. I want to get out of the store fast, but I'm too weak to move.

"You really like it, Doris?" Yolanda unlatches the flap on the purse and takes out the crumpled paper in it. She reaches into her pocket for a fistful of candy. "Want some?" In one motion she has stuffed the little bag into her coat pocket.

"Yolanda. . . ." I finally begin to feel my legs under me. I am moving back, away from the scene that starts happening really fast in front of me, as if someone had yelled "Action!" on a movie set. Yolanda is standing there eating candy. I am moving backward even as she tries to hand me some. A man in a gray suit is moving toward her. I am now behind a rack of purses. I smell the leather. It reminds me of my father's drums that he used to let me play when I was little. Yolanda looks around, but she can't see me. I'm still moving back toward the light of the door. I know that I can't act scared, that I shouldn't run. People look at me. I know they can see me. I know where my arms are, where my legs are, where my head is. I am out on the street in the sun. A woman with a baby carriage bumps into me and says, "Excuse me!" She can see me! I hear a police car siren getting louder as I hurry across the street. I walk faster and faster until I am running and the world is going by so fast that I can't tell what anyone else is doing. I only hear my heart pounding in my chest.

When I crash through the door at home, Mami comes out of the bedroom looking like she just woke up from a deep sleep. I lie down on the sofa. I am sweating and shaking; a sick feeling in my stomach makes me want to curl up. Mami takes my head into her hands. Her fingers are warm and soft. "Are you sick, hija?" I nod my head. Yes. I am sick. I am sick of following Yolanda into trouble. She has problems that make her act crazy. Maybe someday she'll work them out, but I have to start trying to figure out who I am and where I want to go before I can help anybody else. I don't tell my mother any of this. It's better if I just let her take care of me for a little while.

Even as she feels my forehead for fever, my mother can't help humming a tune. It's one I used to know. It's a song about being lonely, even in a crowd, and how that's the way life is for most people. But you have to keep watching out for love because it's out there waiting for you. That's the chorus, I mean. I keep my eyes closed until the words come back to me, until I know it by heart. And I know that I will keep watching but not just watching. Sometimes you have to run fast to catch love because it's hard to see, even when it's right in front of you. I say this to Mami, who laughs and starts really singing. She is really into it now, singing like she was standing in front of hundreds of people in Carnegie Hall, even though I'm the only one here to hear her. The song is for me.

Harriet Tubman: The Road to Freedom

by Rae Bains

When Harriet Tubman was born into slavery in Maryland, she was considered her owner's property, just like his horse or furniture. She endured hardship and brutality before escaping to the North via the Underground Railroad, a network of safe houses for runaway slaves. Called "Moses" after the Bible's freedom leader, she returned many times to help other slaves.

It was beautiful along the eastern shore of Maryland's Chesapeake Bay. The waters were filled with fish, oysters, and clams. In the woods lived rabbits, woodchucks, muskrats, deer, and squirrels. Corn, tobacco, wheat, and vegetables grew in the rich soil.

Maryland was a fine place to live during the early 1800s— if you were free. Ben Ross and Harriet Green were not. They were the slaves of a plantation owner named Edward Brodas. They worked in his fields, cut his lumber, and were his house servants. They did anything he ordered them to do, and their children did the same.

Slaves were called "chattel." That meant they were pieces of property, like sheep or furniture or bales of cotton. The slaves knew that they could be sold at any time. They knew that their children could be taken from them and sent far, far away, and that they could be beaten or whipped. And they knew that their masters would never be punished, for slaves had no rights. They were not allowed any kind of education; they were not even allowed to attend church.

This was the sort of world into which Harriet Ross was born, around 1820. She was the sixth of eleven children born to Ben Ross and Harriet Green. They all lived in a tiny, one-room shack. It had a dirt floor, no windows, and no furniture.

There were no beds. The whole family slept on rags and straw spread on the floor. There were no dishes. The slaves' food—mostly corn mush—was eaten right from the pot it was cooked in. They would scoop it out with a piece of flat stone or an oyster shell. And when they ate, they had to stand or sit on the hard ground.

Slave children had almost no time to play. They were put to work as soon as possible, to "earn their keep." When Harriet was still a very small child, she began running errands for Mr. Brodas and his family. She carried messages as far as ten miles away, going over back roads, through woods, and along river banks.

The only tenderness in Harriet's life came from her family. They gave her so much love that she always had something wonderful to hold on to, even at the worst of times. And one day—many years later—Harriet would thank her parents in the best way she could. She would rescue them, plus six of her brothers and one sister, from slavery, taking them north to freedom.

Soon after she turned five, Harriet was given a new task. Mrs. Brodas put her to work in the mansion, called the "big house." The little girl didn't know a thing about housework. She had never even been inside a real house before—only in the one-room slave shacks—and to make things worse, nobody showed her how to do the things she was supposed to do in the mansion.

So it was no surprise when Harriet made all kinds of mistakes. And when she made mistakes, she was punished.

When Harriet was six, she was sent to live with a family of weavers named Cook. Their home was many miles from the Brodas plantation. Harriet hated being so far from her family, but the Brodases wanted her to learn weaving. Then she would be able to weave for the Brodas family. So, like it or not, Harriet went.

Life with the Cooks was no better than it had been on the Brodas plantation. But Harriet did not stay with the Cooks long. One day, even though she was very sick with measles, Mr. Cook sent her down to the river. She was told to check his muskrat traps. To do this, she had to wade through ice-cold, fast-flowing waters.

The next day, Harriet began to shake and cough. Soon she was burning with fever and could not do any work. She lay in a corner, feeling terrible. Word of her illness quickly passed from one slave to the next, until it reached Harriet's mother.

She begged Mr. Brodas to bring her little girl home. Mr. Brodas agreed. He didn't want to pay the Cooks for teaching someone who was too sick to learn anything, so he had Harriet brought home. There, her mother nursed the little girl back to health.

Harriet's next job was looking after Mrs. Brodas's baby. Here is how Harriet talked about it years later: "I was only seven years old when I was sent to take care of the baby. I was so little I had to sit on the floor and have the baby put in my lap. And that baby was always in my lap except when it was asleep or its mother was feeding it."

Handling such a big responsibility was hard for young Harriet. She never had any time to play or be by herself. She was constantly watched by Mr. and Mrs. Brodas, and they were very strict with her. If she misbehaved, Harriet knew she would be given a whipping. This kind of punishment was used all the time. The owners wanted to keep their slaves frightened, and they did not want the slaves to speak up or fight back—or try to escape.

But the owners could not break the spirit of the slaves.

There always were slaves who stood up for their rights. They bravely held religious services, even though that was forbidden, and they studied reading and writing in secret. They hid and fed other slaves who were trying to escape to the North.

And every year there were slave uprisings. The plantation owners tried to keep the news of these revolts from getting out. They didn't want their own slaves to hear of them, since they might want to do the same thing. But word still passed from one slave to another, from one plantation to another all over the South. It didn't matter that the owners told each other—and the rest of the world—that the slaves were content. The slaves knew better.

Harriet's mother was worried about her. If Harriet angered Mr. Brodas or his wife, they might sell Harriet down the river. Selling someone down the river meant selling that person to a slave trader who would take his new slave down to the Deep South to be put to work in the rice or cotton fields. Life was hard for a slave in Maryland, but it was ten times harder in the Deep South.

Because Mrs. Brodas did not like Harriet's proud, defiant looks, she decided to break the child's spirit. To do so, she hired out the nine-year-old girl to another family in the county. These people made her work all day, cleaning house. Then she had to work at night, caring for a baby. For no reason she was punished every day, and she was fed only enough food to keep her alive.

After a while, Harriet was little more than skin and bones. She was not able to work anymore. Now, sure that she was "broken," the family sent Harriet back to the Brodas plantation. Her body *was* weak and weary, but not her spirit. That was still strong.

Harriet's parents did their best to help her get well. Her mother nursed her every free moment she had. And Ben taught her all kinds of amazing and useful things. Even though he had never gone to school, Ben was a very wise man. He knew a lot about nature. He could tell that it would be a hard winter when the animals grew thicker coats in the fall, he knew where the fishing was good, and he knew which wild plants were safe to eat. As soon as Harriet was up and about, he took her on Sunday-afternoon walks in the woods and along the river.

Part of Harriet's strength came from her brothers and sisters. After a day of working in the fields under a boiling sun, they came back to the shack and brought her all the news of the day. They sang songs and told stories. They told jokes to make her laugh. They did everything they could to make their little sister happy.

Another part of Harriet's strength came from her faith. The slaves were not allowed to have a real church, but they were very religious and held services every Sunday morning. On every plantation there usually was at least one slave who could read or knew the Bible very well. And from this person all the other slaves learned Bible stories and prayers.

Of all the stories in the Bible, the one the slaves liked most was about Moses, who had led the Israelites from slavery. The slaves prayed for a Moses of their own, someone who would lead them to freedom.

Harriet believed deeply that the burden on her people would be eased and that they were meant to be free. She believed what the Bible said: that all people were equal in the eyes of God.

In the next three years, Harriet grew stronger in body and faith. As soon as she was completely well, Mr. Brodas hired her out to another master. This one had her do work hard enough for a grown man. She split rails with an axe, hauled wood, and did other heavy jobs. It was difficult but she never gave up, even when it seemed too much to bear.

By the time she was 11, Harriet was muscular and very strong. She could work as hard and as long as any grownup. Mr. Brodas saw this and put her to work in the fields. Like all the other women in the fields, Harriet wore a bandanna—a large handkerchief—on her head. For the rest of her life she would always wear a bandanna. It was to remind her of her days as a slave, and how far from the fields she had come.

In 1831, new, harsher laws were passed. Now slaves were not allowed to gather in groups. They were not supposed to talk while they worked, and they were never to be on the public roads without a pass from their masters. And the old rules were made stricter. All of this happened because of an uprising led by a man named Nat Turner.

Nat Turner was a slave from Virginia. In the summer of 1831, this man—called the Prophet—led about 70 slaves in a bloody revolt. It took armed troops to stop the revolt and three full months to capture Turner.

The slave owners were scared. If a revolt could happen in Virginia, it could happen anywhere. This fear haunted them more and more, which is why they made stricter laws for the slaves.

But Nat Turner had lit the flame of freedom in many slaves. Harriet was one of these. "I feel just like Nat Turner did," she said one night to her family. "It's better to be dead than a slave."

"It's better to be alive and free," said her brother William.

"And how do we get that?" Harriet asked him. "You know Mr. Brodas won't ever give us our freedom."

"I'm not talking about what he gives," William told her. "I'm talking about what we take for ourselves—like a ride to freedom on the underground railroad."

"What's that?" Harriet wanted to know.

William told Harriet the story of Tice Davids, a slave in Kentucky who ran away. When the plantation owner found out that Davids was gone, he set out after him. Davids swam across the Ohio River with the owner rowing close behind. By the time the owner's boat landed, there was no trace of Tice Davids. It was as if he had vanished into thin air.

The runaway was being helped by people who hated slavery. But the plantation owner knew only that he had vanished. When the slave owner returned, he told everybody that "Tice Davids disappeared so fast, he must have gone on an underground road."

This story was repeated again and again. Soon slaves were

talking about the wonderful secret passage to freedom. Of course, there was no underground road or tunnel from the South to the North. But the slaves kept telling the story anyway. It gave them hope.

Around this time the first railroads were being built in the United States. Trains were the fastest way of traveling that anyone had ever seen. Soon, people were talking about the "underground railroad" that took runaway slaves quickly and safely to the North.

The truth had nothing to do with trains and underground tunnels. The truth was that there were good people who risked their lives to help slaves escape. Some of them hid runaways in their cellars, barns, attics, or in secret rooms in their houses.

These brave people were called "stationmasters." The hiding places were called "depots" or "stations." Other people took the runaways from one depot to another in a hay wagon, on horseback, or on foot. These people were called "conductors." The runaways themselves were known as "passengers" or "parcels." A child was a "small parcel," and a grownup was a "large parcel."

After William told Harriet about the underground railroad, she thought about it all the time. *Maybe,* she told herself, *I'll take that ride to freedom. Maybe all of us will.* It was this hope that kept Harriet going.

When Harriet was 15 her hope—and her life—almost ended. One September evening she was sent to the village store. While she was there another slave hurried in. He belonged to a farmer named Barrett. A moment later Barrett rushed in.

"Get back to the field!" Barrett shouted at the slave.

The slave just stared back silently. Nobody else in the store made a move.

"I'll whip you," Barrett threatened.

The slave began to edge away. "Stop!" Barrett yelled.

"You," Barrett said, pointing at Harriet and a young boy next to her. "Hold him so I can tie him up."

Harriet didn't obey the order. And she kept the boy from doing anything.

Suddenly, the slave ran to the door. Barrett leaped to the store counter and picked up a heavy lead weight. He whirled and threw the weight at the runaway. But it missed the man. The heavy piece of metal struck Harriet in the head. She fell to the floor, unconscious.

For the next couple of months Harriet lay near death. At first, she couldn't eat. She grew thinner and thinner and slept most of the time. Her wound was healing slowly, but there was a very deep cut in her forehead. It left a scar she would carry for the rest of her life.

Mr. Brodas was sure Harriet was going to die, so he tried to sell her. Time after time he brought slave buyers to the shack, where Harriet lay on a pile of rags. But each time the buyer's answer was the same: "Even if she lives, she'll never be able to put in a day's work. I wouldn't give you a penny for her."

Winter came, and Harriet was still alive. Her parents were thankful but still worried about her. Harriet could walk and talk and do light chores around the shack. But sometimes, in the middle of whatever she was doing, Harriet fell asleep.

It could happen even while she was saying something. She would simply stop talking, close her eyes, and sleep for a few minutes. Then she would wake up and go on talking as if no time had passed.

The Brodas family was sure that Harriet's "spells" meant she was half-witted, so they tried that much harder to sell her. But Harriet did not want to be sold and sent away from her family. And she certainly was not half-witted; she was a very clever 15-year-old.

Every time Mr. Brodas came to the shack with a buyer, Harriet made believe that she was having one of her spells, or she acted very, very stupid. Her family and friends went along with Harriet's play-acting, and nobody was ever interested in buying her.

In time, Harriet's strength returned. She could lift huge,

heavy barrels. She could pull a loaded wagon for miles. She drove the oxen in the fields and plowed from morning to night. It was said that she was stronger than the strongest man in Maryland. It was a strength she would need in the days to come.

Harriet's dream of freedom was still alive. But she had to put it off for a while. In 1844, she married a free black man named John Tubman. She hoped that he would help her get away to the North. But the marriage was not happy, and they soon parted. Harriet continued to use the name of Tubman.

Not long after that, word reached the Brodas slaves that many of them were going to be sold. Harriet knew the time had come to make the break for freedom. She turned for help to a white woman who lived nearby. This woman had once told Harriet, "If you ever need anything, come to me." Harriet knew that meant helping her to escape.

Without telling anyone, Harriet set out for Bucktown, where the white woman lived. When she reached the house, Harriet said to the woman, "You told me to come when I needed your help. I need it now."

The woman gave Harriet a paper with two names on it, and directions how she might get to the first house where she would receive aid.

When Harriet reached this first house, she showed the woman of the house the paper. Harriet was told to take a broom and sweep the yard. In this way, anyone passing the house would not suspect the young woman working in the yard of being a runaway slave.

The woman's husband, who was a farmer, came home in the early evening. In the dark he loaded a wagon, put Harriet in it, well covered, and drove to the outskirts of another town. Here he told her to get out and directed her to a second "station."

Harriet was passed along this way, from station to station. She was riding the underground railroad, and she didn't stop until she crossed into Pennsylvania. Now she was free at last! As she remembered years later, "When I found I had crossed that line, I looked at my hands to see if I was the same person. There was such a glory over everything. The sun came like gold through the trees, and over the fields, and I felt like I was in heaven."

But Harriet's "heaven" wasn't perfect. "I was free," she said, "but there was no one to welcome me to the land of freedom. I was a stranger in a strange land. And my home, after all, was down in Maryland, because my father, my mother, my brothers, my sisters, and friends were there. But I was free, and they should be free! I would make a home in the North and bring them there."

In the next few years, Harriet did what she swore she would do. She made trip after trip to the South, risking her life to bring others to freedom. She rescued her family, friends, other slaves—more than 300 men, women, and children.

Harriet was loved by the slaves. They called her their "Moses," because she led them through the wilderness and out of bondage. And she was hated by the slave owners, who offered a $40,000 reward for her capture.

Harriet was never caught. She became the most famous conductor on the underground railroad. And, as she said, "I never ran my train off the track, and I never lost a passenger."

The legend of Harriet Tubman grew during the Civil War. Fighting for the Union, she made many raids behind enemy lines as a scout and a spy. And as a nurse, she helped the sick and wounded soldiers, both Northerners and Southerners.

After the Civil War, Harriet made her home in Auburn, New York. But she never stopped doing good works. Until her death, on March 10, 1913, the woman called Moses did many things. She fought for the right of women to vote, she helped create schools for black students, and she did everything she could for the poor, the old, and the helpless.

When Harriet Tubman died, at the age of 93, she was honored with a military funeral. It was a fitting tribute to the woman who fought so many battles for the freedom of her people.

August Heat

by William F. Harvey

Some events are too peculiar and ghostly to be accepted as coincidence. In this story, an English artist believes he sees the future. But is the future as horrible as he imagines?

PHENISTONE ROAD, CLAPHAM
August 20th, 190_.

I have had what I believe to be the most remarkable day in my life, and while the events are still fresh in my mind, I wish to put them down on paper as clearly as possible.

Let me say at the outset that my name is James Clarence Withencroft.

I am 40 years old, in perfect health, never having known a day's illness.

By profession I am an artist, not a very successful one, but I earn enough money by my black-and-white work to satisfy my necessary wants.

My only near relative, a sister, died five years ago, so that I am independent.

I breakfasted this morning at nine, and after glancing through the morning paper I lighted my pipe and proceeded to let my mind wander in the hope that I might chance upon some subject for my pencil.

The room, though door and windows were open, was oppressively hot, and I had just made up my mind that the coolest and most comfortable place in the neighborhood would be the deep end of the public swimming bath, when the idea came.

I began to draw. So intent was I on my work that I left my lunch untouched, only stopping work when the clock of St. Jude's struck four.

The final result, for a hurried sketch, was, I felt sure, the best thing I had done.

It showed a criminal in the dock immediately after the judge had pronounced sentence. The man was fat—enormously fat. The flesh hung in rolls about his chin; it creased his huge, stumpy neck. He was clean shaven (perhaps I should say a few days before he must have been clean shaven) and almost bald. He stood in the dock, his short, clumsy fingers clasping the rail, looking straight in front of him. The feeling that his expression conveyed was not so much one of horror as of utter, absolute collapse.

There seemed nothing in the man strong enough to sustain that mountain of flesh.

I rolled up the sketch, and without quite knowing why, placed it in my pocket. Then with the rare sense of happiness which the knowledge of a good thing well done gives, I left the house.

I believe that I set out with the idea of calling upon Trenton, for I remember walking along Lytton Street and turning to the right along Gilchrist Road at the bottom of the hill, where the men were at work on the new tram lines.

From there onwards I have only the vaguest recollection of where I went. The one thing of which I was fully conscious was the awful heat, that came up from the dusty asphalt pavements as an almost palpable wave. I longed for the thunder promised by the great banks of copper-colored cloud that hung low over the western sky.

I must have walked five or six miles, when a small boy roused me from my reverie by asking the time.

It was 20 minutes to seven.

When he left me I began to take stock of my bearings. I found myself standing before a gate that led into a yard bordered by a strip of thirsty earth, where there were flowers, purple stock and scarlet geranium. Above the entrance was a board with the inscription—

CHS. ATKINSON.   MONUMENTAL MASON.

WORKER IN ENGLISH AND ITALIAN MARBLES

From the yard itself came a cheery whistle, the noise of hammer blows, and the cold sound of steel meeting stone.

A sudden impulse made me enter.

A man was sitting with his back towards me, busy at work on a slab of curiously veined marble. He turned round as he heard my steps and I stopped short.

It was the man I had been drawing, whose portrait lay in my pocket.

He sat there, huge and elephantine, the sweat pouring from his scalp, which he wiped with a red silk handkerchief. But though the face was the same, the expression was absolutely different.

He greeted me smiling, as if we were old friends, and shook my hand.

I apologized for my intrusion.

"Everything is hot and glary outside," I said. "This seems an oasis in the wilderness."

"I don't know about the oasis," he replied, "but it certainly is hot, as hot as hell. Take a seat, sir!"

He pointed to the end of the gravestone on which he was at work, and I sat down.

"That's a beautiful piece of stone you've got hold of," I said.

He shook his head. "In a way it is," he answered; "the surface here is as fine as anything you could wish, but there's a big flaw at the back, though I don't expect you'd ever notice it. I could never make really a good job of a bit of marble like that. It would be all right in the summer like this; it wouldn't mind the blasted heat. But wait till the winter comes. There's nothing quite like frost to find out the weak points in stone."

"Then what's it for?" I asked.

The man burst out laughing.

"You'd hardly believe me if I was to tell you it's for an exhibition, but it's the truth. Artists have exhibitions: so do grocers and butchers; we have them too. All the latest little things in headstones, you know."

He went on to talk of marbles, which sort best withstood wind and rain, and which were easiest to work; then of his garden and a new sort of carnation he had bought. At the end of every other minute he would drop his tools, wipe his shining head, and curse the heat.

I said little, for I felt uneasy. There was something unnatural, uncanny, in meeting this man.

I tried at first to persuade myself that I had seen him before, that his face, unknown to me, had found a place in some out-of-the-way corner of my memory, but I knew that I was practicing little more than a plausible piece of self-deception.

Mr. Atkinson finished his work, spat on the ground, and got up with a sigh of relief.

"There! What do you think of that?" he said, with an air of evident pride.

The inscription which I read for the first time was this—

SACRED TO THE MEMORY

OF

JAMES CLARENCE WITHENCROFT.

BORN JAN. 18TH, 1860.

HE PASSED AWAY VERY SUDDENLY

ON AUGUST 20TH, 190—

"In the midst of life we are in death."

For the first time I sat in silence. Then a cold shudder ran down my spine. I asked him where he had seen the name.

"Oh, I didn't see it anywhere," replied Mr. Atkinson. "I wanted some name, and I put down the first that came into my head. Why do you want to know?"

"It's a strange coincidence, but it happens to be mine."

He gave a long, low whistle.

"And the dates?"

"I can only answer for one of them, and that's correct."

"It's a rum go!" he said.

But he knew less than I did. I told him of my morning's work. I took the sketch from my pocket and showed it to him. As he looked, the expression of his face altered until it became more and more like that of the man I had drawn.

"And it was only the day before yesterday," he said, "that I told Maria there were no such things as ghosts!"

Neither of us had seen a ghost, but I knew what he meant.

"You probably heard my name," I said.

"And you must have seen me somewhere and have forgotten it! Were you at Clacton-on-Sea last July?"

I had never been to Clacton in my life. We were silent for some time. We were both looking at the same thing, the two dates on the gravestone, and one was right.

"Come inside and have some supper," said Mr. Atkinson.

His wife was a cheerful little woman, with the flaky red cheeks of the countrybred. Her husband introduced me as a friend of his who was an artist. The result was unfortunate, for after the sardines and watercress had been removed, she brought out a Doré Bible, and I had to sit and express my admiration for nearly half an hour.

I went outside, and found Atkinson sitting on the gravestone smoking.

We resumed the conversation at the point we had left off.

"You must excuse my asking," I said, "but do you know of anything you've done for which you could be put on trial?"

He shook his head.

"I'm not bankrupt, the business is prosperous enough. Three years ago I gave turkeys to some of the guardians at Christmas, but that's all I can think of. And they were small ones, too," he added as an afterthought.

He got up, fetched a can from the porch, and began to water the flowers. "Twice a day regular in the hot weather," he said, "and then the heat sometimes gets the better of the delicate ones. And ferns, good Lord! they could never stand it. Where do you live?"

I told him my address. It would take an hour's quick walk to get back home.

"It's like this," he said. "We'll look at the matter straight. If you go back home tonight, you take your chance of accidents. A cart may run over you, and there's always banana skins and orange peel, to say nothing of fallen ladders."

He spoke of the improbable with an intense seriousness that would have been laughable six hours before. But I did not laugh.

"The best thing we can do," he continued, "is for you to stay here till 12 o'clock. We'll go upstairs and smoke; it may be cooler inside."

To my surprise, I agreed.

We are sitting now in a long, low room beneath the eaves. Atkinson has sent his wife to bed. He himself is busy sharpening some tools at a little oilstone, smoking one of my cigars the while.

The air seems charged with thunder. I am writing this at a shaky table before the open window. The leg is cracked, and Atkinson, who seems a handy man with his tools, is going to mend it as soon as he has finished putting an edge on his chisel.

It is after 11 now. I shall be gone in less than an hour.

But the heat is stifling.

It is enough to send a man mad.

Lineage

by Margaret Walker

My grandmothers were strong.
They followed plows and bent to toil.
They moved through fields sowing seed.
They touched earth and grain grew.
They were full of sturdiness and singing.
My grandmothers were strong.

My grandmothers are full of memories.
Smelling of soap and onions and wet clay
With veins rolling roughly over quick hands
They have many clean words to say.
My grandmothers were strong.
Why am I not as they?

A Special Gift

by Miriam Rinn

Before the fall of communism, religion was discouraged in the Soviet Union. Jews, especially, were condemned if they wanted to practice their faith openly. Many of the Soviet Jews who immigrated to the United States in the 70s and 80s knew little about Jewish holidays and customs.

Marci pushed aside her English as a Second Language book, and stretched her arms high over her head. Getting up from the table, she went to look out the window of the small living room. She had lived in the United States for 11 months now, and in Fair Lawn for eight, and the courtyard of the garden apartment complex still looked strange to her. It was nothing like the park across the street from their building in Moscow. There she had played with her friends and walked with Mama and Papa and Alex after dinner and on Sundays. Here, most of the girls in school lived in large houses and no one walked for pleasure, except for people walking their dogs or ladies getting their exercise.

Marci chewed her bottom lip. Of course, here they had a car, even though Mama complained that it would not last the winter, and Alex had a chance to go to the best college. It didn't matter that he was Jewish; it only mattered that he was smart. That was why he studied all the time, and why he had to have the small bedroom. Marci had to sleep on the couch. She didn't mind. She could get up very early on Saturday mornings and watch cartoons, if she kept the sound low. Some of them didn't seem funny to her, but the commercials were wonderful. So many toys and cereals!

As Marci shifted her weight to the other foot, she saw a bulky shape cautiously descend the few steps to the sidewalk. Mrs. Gold, the elderly woman who lived in the next apartment, was walking her dog, Trixie. Marci giggled when she remembered Papa's remark that Trixie was almost as old and slow as Mrs. Gold. It was true, but Marci was fond of them both. They were the only living things she saw regularly in the courtyard.

Marci glanced quickly at the clock on the wall. It was only 4:30 P.M. She had time to talk to Mrs. Gold before she put the soup on to warm. Mama and Papa didn't come home until 6 P.M., and Alex was going to the library to study.

She slid into her coat and gloves and grabbed a scarf on the way out the door. "Mrs. Gold," she called. "Wait. I'll walk with you."

"Why, hello, Masha. How nice to have company." Mrs. Gold smiled warmly. She wasn't much taller than Marci. "What happened to your beautiful blonde braids? You have a new hairdo."

"Mama's girlfriend Vera cut it and gave me a perm." Marci patted her crimped hair. "Do you think I look good?" she asked shyly.

Mrs. Gold put a gloved hand around her shoulder and squeezed. "You look very fashionable, very American."

Marci took a deep, happy breath. "And call me Marci, with an *i*, not Masha."

Mrs. Gold laughed. "What are you doing for Hanukkah, Marci? Any big plans? My daughter invited me to her house for a week."

Marci was quiet. She had heard the children in class talking about Hanukkah. They seemed very excited about all the gifts they expected. When she asked Mama about this, Mama had said she thought it was some sort of Jewish holiday, but she wasn't sure. Anyway, they were so busy at the discount store where she worked that she didn't have the time or strength to prepare for any holiday. And Marci knew there was no money for presents. Alex had said that he wasn't interested in Jewish holidays. Being a Jew had already cost him his spot at the Moscow Polytechnic Institute, and that was quite enough.

Marci looked down at her shoes. "I don't know, Mrs. Gold. What are you supposed to do on Hanukkah?"

They stopped walking to wait for Trixie, who had sat down to rest. "You don't know? Oy, what a shame!" Mrs. Gold clucked sympathetically.

"It's different in Russia," Marci explained. "No one talks about being Jewish. It's as if it's a terrible secret that you can't let anyone know."

"Well, you light candles and sing songs," Mrs. Gold told Marci, "and you play with a spinning top called a dreidel. And you eat latkes—potato pancakes, of course, with applesauce or sour cream. And someone tells the story of what happened to the Maccabees long ago. When I was young all the grown-ups gave the children coins, Hanukkah gelt, but now I think they get presents. I still give my grandchildren money though."

"It sounds like a party," said Marci, smiling.

They began to walk again and Mrs. Gold leaned on Marci for support. "That's what people do." Mrs. Gold nodded. "Jewish people, Marci, like you."

Marci imagined being at a party, all the people laughing and singing. Candles would be burning, and Papa and Alex would be trying to beat each other at chess. Vera would tell naughty jokes that would make Mama's eyes tear from laughing, while her husband, Misha, would blush. Marci would read the story of Hanukkah. And everyone there would be happy they were Jewish.

Marci looked seriously at the old woman. "Will you help me, Mrs. Gold, to make a party for my family? A real Hanukkah party?"

"Of course I'll help you, darling. It would be my pleasure. You'll need a menorah and candles, a book that tells the story, a dreidel, and what else? Let's see . . . ."

While Mrs. Gold thought, Marci figured quickly. It would cost a lot of money to buy all the things she needed, and she didn't have any money. She certainly couldn't ask Mama or Alex. She wanted the party to be a surprise, a Hanukkah gift for her family. She would have to earn the money somehow.

"I need a job, Mrs. Gold. Could I walk Trixie for you now that it's cold? She likes me." Marci bent down quickly to pet the old dog. She hoped Mrs. Gold wouldn't be angry.

"What a wonderful idea! If you could walk Trixie twice a day, and help me get out too, I'll be happy to pay $10 a week. How's that?" Mrs. Gold asked.

"Oh, that's a lot of money. Mama will be angry."

"Mama doesn't have to know. She leaves for work around 7 A.M., right? You can walk Trixie at 7:30 A.M. and when you come home from school. Is it a deal?" Mrs. Gold stuck out her hand.

Marci took it and shook it vigorously, just as people did at home. "It's a deal."

Marci had been walking Trixie for two weeks and she had $20 saved. She had spent hours making potato pancakes in Mrs. Gold's apartment. Today, she and Mrs. Gold were walking to town to buy all the things they needed. Tomorrow night was the first night of Hanukkah and her party.

Marci folded the two ten-dollar bills carefully and put them in her pocket. "Mrs. Gold, are you ready?" she called through the door impatiently. "It's time to go."

The door opened. Mrs. Gold was pinning her hat to her head. "I'm coming, I'm coming. I can't move as fast as you." Mrs. Gold locked the door and tucked her arm through

Marci's. Slowly, they began their six-block walk to town. "We'll go to the Jewish book store first. They should have a menorah, candles, and a book about Hanukkah. Then we'll stop at the grocery and get applesauce and sour cream. I have everything I need to make cookies before my grandson picks me up tomorrow. I even have a cookie cutter shaped like a dreidel. So we're all set."

When Marci saw the line of shops, her heart began to beat more quickly. It seemed as if it was taking them forever to get to town. Finally, they stopped in front of a small store with many books in the window. There were silver and brass objects and banners of shiny fabric.

Marci suddenly felt shy and hesitant. She didn't know what any of the objects in the shop window were, or what the strange letters meant. She wouldn't know what to ask for, and the people in the shop would think she was foolish. Maybe she had made a mistake. "I don't know, Mrs. Gold. Maybe we should go home. In Russia, being a Jew only gave trouble. Alex will say I'm a fool."

Mrs. Gold's voice became serious. "In America, Marci, there is nothing wrong with being Jewish, or being Christian, or being Buddhist, or being nothing. Everyone can believe whatever he wants, as long as he doesn't bother other people from believing what they want." Her voice softened. "Now you have a chance to find out how lucky you are to be a part of such an amazing people. Come, I'll help you find everything you need to make a wonderful Hanukkah party."

Taking a deep breath of the cold evening air, Marci pulled open the door. Soon, she was deciding between a wood or a brass menorah, a dreidel filled with chocolates that didn't spin very well or one without candy that spun for a full 30 seconds, a blue-and-white or a multi-colored HAPPY HANUKKAH banner, napkins with pictures of dreidels or a decorated table-cloth made of paper. There were also paper plates and cups with Hanukkah decorations on them, and dozens of other things she wanted to buy.

"So, young lady," said the man behind the counter. "What will it be?"

Marci clutched the money in her pocket. "I want the wooden menorah, this dreidel without the candy, the table-cloth, and this sign. How much will it cost?"

"And put in a box of candles," Mrs. Gold added.

The man gathered all the items together and went to the cash register. "It's $16.73 altogether."

Marci let out her breath in relief. She had enough for applesauce and sour cream, too.

It was when they were standing in front of the grocery that Marci remembered. "Mrs. Gold, we didn't buy a book, a book that tells about the holiday!"

"You're right, and now all the money is gone."

Marci's thoughts raced. Where could she get a book? If they couldn't read about what had happened to the Jews thousands of years ago, it wouldn't be a real Hanukkah party. No one in her family would understand what they were celebrating.

Marci looked at her watch. It was already 5:20 P.M. "We could go quickly to the library, Mrs. Gold. Mama and Papa don't get home until six."

"That's a good idea, Marci, but you go by yourself. I'll never make it that far. I'm already tired and cold."

Marci hesitated. She could get to the library and home if she ran all the way. But what about Mrs. Gold? It was dark, and she didn't walk steadily without help.

"No, it doesn't matter. We will go home now together."

It seemed to Marci that Mrs. Gold gave a sigh of relief as she took Marci's arm, but Marci was too miserable to care much. Her parents and Alex and Vera and Misha would eat the potato pancakes and the cookies shaped like dreidels, but they wouldn't know why, and Marci wouldn't be able to explain. She couldn't remember what the marks on the dreidel meant, or how the game was played. She'd never be able to remember what to say when she lit the candle, or the name of the bad king, or when it happened or where. Her family would have a good time, but it wouldn't be special. It wouldn't be a Hanukkah party.

Marci added the last of the pancakes to the tray in the oven and checked the clock. Vera and her husband would be arriving soon. She'd told them to come a little before 6:00 P.M. Mama and Papa were coming home at the usual time, and Alex had promised to come back in time.

She looked around the small apartment and made sure everything was ready. The menorah with one candle in the middle and one at the end was sitting on top of the TV. The dreidel was right next to it. Marci had tacked the banner over the kitchen door so everybody could see it as soon as they came in. The tablecloth was spread, and the table was set. Everything looked pretty, but Marci felt as if a stone was on her chest, preventing her from breathing freely. If only she'd remembered to buy the book, she'd have been glad to use a plain tablecloth.

The knock at the door startled Marci. Could Vera be here already? She was always late.

When Marci opened the door, she saw Mrs. Gold holding a plate full of dreidel-shaped cookies and a package wrapped in blue-and-white paper. "I'm sorry I couldn't come earlier, darling, but my grandson just arrived, and he was bringing me something I needed. Here are the cookies, and here is something special for you. Remember, I said I still give Hanukkah gelt, but this time I made an exception. Go, open it. I have to go in a minute."

Marci took the plate of cookies and placed it on the table. Then she turned her attention to the package. Mrs. Gold had bought her a Hanukkah present! What could it be?

Marci pulled off the white ribbon and pulled apart the gift paper. She gasped when she saw the title of the book. "It's the story of Hanukkah! Now I'll be able to have a real Hanukkah party."

Mrs. Gold laughed and hugged Marci to her. She smelled of

roses and the fur collar on her coat tickled. "Have a wonderful Hanukkah and a beautiful party. You'll tell me all about it when I come home and you take me for my walk."

Just then, Mama walked into the living room. "Mashinka, what's this? Something smells delicious, and the table is so fancy."

"We're having a party, Mama, a Hanukkah party."

"Have a great time, darling." Mrs. Gold hurried out the door. "Happy Hanukkah!"

Father

by Gary Soto

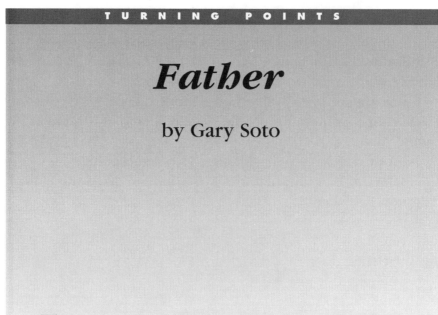

When someone you love dies, it can seem as though the world has stopped. It hasn't, but nothing will ever be exactly the same. In this essay, the author recalls his father's death.

My father was showing me how to water. Earlier in the day he and a friend had leveled the backyard with a roller, then with a two-by-four they dragged on a rope to fill in the depressed areas, after which they watered the ground and combed it slowly with a steel rake. They were preparing the ground for a new lawn. They worked shirtless in the late summer heat, and talked only so often, stopping now and then to point and say things I did not understand—how fruit trees would do better near the alley and how the vegetable garden would do well on the east side of the house.

"Put your thumb like this," he said. Standing over me, he took the hose and placed his thumb over the opening so that the water streamed out hissing and showed silver in that dusk. I tried it and the water hissed and went silver as I pointed the hose to a square patch of dirt that I soaked but was careful not to puddle.

Father returned to sit down with an iced tea. His knees were water-stained and his chest was flecked with mud. Mom sat next to him, garden gloves resting on her lap. She was wearing checkered shorts and her hair was tied up in a bandanna. He patted his lap, and she jumped into it girlishly, arms around his neck. They raised their heads to watch me—or look through me, as if something were on the other side of me—and talked about our new house—the neighbors, trees they would plant, the playground down the block. They were tired from the day's work but were happy. When Father pinched her legs, as if to imply they were fat, she punched him gently and played with his hair.

The water streamed, nickel-colored, as I slowly worked from one end to the next. When I raised my face to Father's to ask if I could stop, he pointed to an area that I had missed. Although it was summer I was cold from the water and my thumb hurt from pressing the hose, triggerlike, to reach the far places. But I wanted to please him, to work hard as he had, so I watered the patch until he told me to stop. I turned off the water, coiled the hose as best I could, and sat with them as they talked about the house and stared at where I had been standing.

The next day Father was hurt at work. A neck injury. Two days later he was dead. I remember the hour—two in the afternoon. An uncle slammed open the back door at Grandma's and the three of us—cousin Isaac, Debbie, and I who were playing in the yard—grew stiff because we thought we were in trouble for doing something wrong. He looked at us, face lined with worry and shouting to hurry to the car. At the hospital I recall Mother holding her hand over her eyes as if she was looking into a light. She was leaning into someone's shoulder and was being led away from the room in which Father lay.

I remember looking up but saying nothing, though I sensed what had happened—that Father was dead. I did not feel sorrow nor did I cry, but I felt conspicuous because relatives were pressing me against their legs or holding my hand or touching my head, tenderly. I stood among them, some of whom were crying while others had their heads bowed and mouths moving. The three of us were led away down the hall to a cafeteria where an uncle bought us candies that we ate standing up and looking around, after which we left the hospital and walked into a harsh afternoon light. We got into a blue car I had never seen before.

At the funeral there was crying. I knelt with my brother and sister, hands folded and trying to be patient, though I was itchy from the tiny coat whose shoulders worked into my armpits and from the heat of a stuffy car on our long and slow drive from the church in town. Prayers were said and a eulogy was given by a man we did not know. We were asked to view the casket, with our mother and the three of us to lead the procession. An uncle helped my mother while we walked shyly to view our father for the last time. When I stood at the casket, I was surprised to see him, eyes closed and moist-looking and wearing a cap the color of skin. (Years later I would realize that it hid the wound from which he had died.) I looked quickly and returned to my seat, head bowed because my relatives were watching me and I felt scared.

We buried our father. Later that day at the house, Grandma could not stop shaking from her nerves, so a doctor was called. I was in the room when he opened his bag and shiny things gleamed from inside it. Scared, I left the room and sat in the living room with my sister, who had a doughnut in her hand, with one bite gone. An aunt whose face was twisted from crying looked at me and, feeling embarrassed, I lowered my head to play with my fingers.

A week later relatives came to help build the fence Father had planned for the new house. A week after that Rick, Debra, and I were playing in an unfurnished bedroom with a can of marbles Mother had given us. Behind the closed door we rolled the marbles so that they banged against the baseboard and jumped into the air. We separated, each to a corner, where we swept them viciously with our arms—the clatter of the marbles hitting the walls so loud I could not hear the things in my heart.

Do Not Go Gentle Into That Good Night

by Dylan Thomas

Do not go gentle into that good night,
Old age should burn and rave at close of day;
Rage, rage against the dying of the light.

Though wise men at their end know dark is right,
Because their words have forked no lightning they
Do not go gentle into that good night.

Good men, the last wave by, crying how bright
Their frail deeds might have danced in a green bay,
Rage, rage against the dying of the light.

Wild men who caught and sang the sun in flight,
And learn, too late, they grieved it on its way,
Do not go gentle into that good night.

Grave men, near death, who see with blinding sight
Blind eyes could blaze like meteors and be gay,
Rage, rage against the dying of the light.

And you, my father, there on the sad height,
Curse, bless, me now with your fierce tears, I pray,
Do not go gentle into that good night.
Rage, rage against the dying of the light.

Shark Bait

by Dave Barry

Here's a look at men and nature from a satirical angle.
Would you like to be out in a boat with these guys
when a shark swims by?

It began as a fun nautical outing, 10 of us in a motorboat off the coast of Miami. The weather was sunny and we saw no signs of danger, other than the risk of sliding overboard because every exposed surface on the boat was covered with a layer of snack-related grease. We had enough cholesterol on board to put the entire U.S. Olympic team into cardiac arrest. This is because all 10 of us were guys.

I hate to engage in gender stereotyping, but when women plan the menu for a recreational outing, they usually come up with a nutritionally balanced menu featuring all the major food groups, including the Sliced Carrots Group, the Pieces of Fruit Cut into Cubes Group, the Utensils Group, and the Plate Group. Whereas guys tend to focus on the Carbonated Malt Beverages Group and the Fatal Snacks Group. On this particular trip, our food supply consisted of about 14 bags of potato chips and one fast-food fried-chicken Giant Economy Tub o' Fat. Nobody brought, for example, napkins, the theory being that you could just wipe your hands on your stomach. Then you could burp. This is what guys on all-guy boats are doing while women are thinking about their relationships.

The reason the grease got smeared everywhere was that four of the guys on the boat were 10-year-olds, who, because of the way their still-developing digestive systems work, cannot chew without punching. This results in a lot of dropped and thrown food. On this boat, you regularly encountered semignawed pieces of chicken skittering across the deck toward you like small but hostile alien creatures from the Kentucky Fried Planet. Periodically a man would yell "CUT THAT OUT!" at the boys, then burp to indicate the depth of his concern. Discipline is vital on a boat.

We motored through random-looking ocean until we found exactly what we were looking for: a patch of random-looking ocean. There we dropped anchor and dove for Florida lobsters, which protect themselves by using their tails to scoot backward really fast. They've been fooling predators with this move for millions of years, but the guys on our boat, being advanced life forms, including a dentist, figured it out in under three hours.

I myself did not participate, because I believe that lobsters are the result of a terrible genetic accident involving nuclear radiation and cockroaches. I mostly sat around, watching guys lunge out of the water, heave lobsters into the boat, burp, and plunge back in. Meanwhile, the lobsters were scrabbling around in the chicken grease, frantically trying to shoot backward through the forest of legs belonging to 10-year-old boys squirting each other with gobs of the No. 197,000,000,000 Sun Block that their moms had sent along. It was a total Guy Day, very relaxing, until the arrival of the barracuda.

This occurred just after we'd all gotten out of the water. One of the men, Larry, was fishing, and he hooked a barracuda right where we had been swimming. This was unsettling. The books all say that barracuda rarely eat people, but very few barracuda can read, and they have *far* more teeth than would be necessary for a strictly seafood diet. Their mouths look like the entire $39.95 set of Ginsu knives, including the handy Arm Slicer.

We gathered around to watch Larry fight the barracuda. His plan was to catch it, weigh it, and release it with a warning. After 10 minutes he almost had it to the boat, and we were all pretty excited for him, when all of a sudden...

Ba-Dump...Ba-Dump...

Those of you who you read music recognize this as the soundtrack from the motion picture *Jaws*. Sure enough, cruising right behind Larry's barracuda, thinking sushi, was: a shark. And not just any shark. It was a hammerhead shark, perennial winner of the coveted Oscar for Ugliest Fish. It has a weird, T-shaped head with a big eyeball on each tip, so that it can see around both sides of a telephone pole. This ability is of course useless for a fish, but nobody would dare to try to explain this to a hammerhead.

The hammerhead, its fin breaking the surface, zig-zagged closer to Larry's barracuda, then surged forward.

"Oh ****!" went Larry, reeling furiously.

CHOMP went the hammerhead, and suddenly Larry's barracuda was in a new weight division.

CHOMP went the hammerhead again, and now Larry was competing in an entirely new category, Fish Consisting of Only a Head.

The boys were staring at the remainder of the barracuda, deeply impressed.

"This is your leg," said the dentist. "This is your leg in *Jaws*. Any questions?"

The boys, for the first time all day, were quiet.

The Mad Yak

by Gregory Corso

I am watching them churn the last milk
    they'll ever get from me.
They are waiting for me to die;
They want to make buttons out of my bones.
Where are my sisters and brothers?
That tall monk there, loading my uncle,
    he has a new cap.
And that idiot student of his—
    I never saw that muffler before.
Poor uncle, he lets them load him.
How sad he is, how tired!
I wonder what they'll do with his bones?
And that beautiful tail!
How many shoelaces will they make of that!

Dancing Drum

by Terri Cohlene

*The Cherokee people tell of a time when souls could
still return from the Land of the Spirits. It was then that
a boy's momentary mistake changed human life
forever.*

One day long ago, when souls could still return from the
Land of the Spirits, the Sun looked down upon the
Earth. "The People of the Mountain do not like me," she
said to her brother, the Moon. "See how they twist up their faces
when they look to the sky."

"Ah, but they love me," replied the Moon. "They smile when
they see me, and they make music and dance and send me
songs." This did not please the Sun, for she thought she was
more important than her brother and more deserving.

That night, as she always did, the Sun visited her daughter
for the evening meal. "How can The People love my brother
and not me?" she asked. "I will show them it is unwise to offend
me!" And the next morning, followed by the next and the next,
she sent scorching heat onto the land.

During this time of the angry Sun, there lived in a small Cherokee village a boy named Dancing Drum. He saw the suffering of his people. The crops no longer flourished, the children no longer laughed, the old women no longer gossiped, and the river, Long Man, was drying up. Soon there would be no water even for drinking.

Dancing Drum went to the Shaman and asked, "Why is Grandmother Sun burning the land and The People? How can we make her stop?"

The Shaman drank the last drop of water from her drinking gourd. "I do not know," she said. "But in a dream, a woodpecker came to me and told me to go to the little men in the wood. Alas, I have grown too weak to travel. You are young and strong. It is up to you to go."

Honored to be chosen for such an important mission, Dancing Drum followed the Shaman's directions and soon found the little men in the wood. "How can we make Grandmother Sun stop burning The People?" he asked them.

"You must go to the Land of the Sky People and kill the Sun before she destroys us all," they said. "First, take these snake rattles and tie them onto your moccasins."

As soon as he did this, Dancing Drum felt a strange tingling from his heels to his head. Suddenly he could not move his arms, and when he tried to move his legs, he only heard the shaking of the rattles. He called for help. "Hssssssss!" was all he could say, for he had become a snake!

"Do not worry," said the leader of the little men. "You will be yourself again when your task is complete." He pointed to a small opening in the underbrush. "Now follow this path to the house of the Sun's daughter. In the morning, when the Sun comes out, bite her quickly."

Soon Dancing Drum became used to the sidewinding movements of his new body. He slithered along the path into the woods, up the tallest mountain, and through the mist to the clouds themselves. At last he came upon a large domed house made of mud and cane. It was the house of the Sun's daughter.

Since it was near dawn, Dancing Drum hid behind the clay pots stacked outside the door. I'll catch the Sun as she comes out, he thought. But when the door opened, she rushed by him so quickly, he didn't even have time to strike.

He would have to be more alert next time. He slept throughout the day, and as twilight approached, Dancing Drum was ready. This time, when the Sun drew near, he tensed to spring at her. But at the last instant he turned away, blinded for a moment by her brilliance.

I must try again, he vowed, and this time I will not miss. Through the night he waited. As soon as he heard stirrings from inside the house, he slithered to the door and closed his eyes.

"Forgive me, Grandmother Sun," he hissed. A moment later, the door opened and Dancing Drum struck. He felt his fangs sink deep into her ankle. But when he looked, he saw that it was not the Sun but her daughter who lay dead on the ground.

Just then, Dancing Drum shed his scaly skin. He was a boy once more. With the Sun's wail filling the air, he ran from the Land of the Sky People. Over the clouds he went, through the mist, and down the tallest mountain. After many days he reached his village.

There the chief was holding counsel. "At last we have relief from Grandmother Sun's burning heat," he said. "But in her sadness over the death of her daughter, she no longer leaves her house." He pulled his robe tighter around his shoulders. "Now The People are cold and in darkness."

Stepping into the chief's circle, Dancing Drum announced, "I am the cause of this darkness. I stopped the heat, but our suffering grows worse. I will go to the Land of the Spirits and bring back the Daughter of the Sun. Then our grandmother will once again smile upon The People."

Once more, Dancing Drum consulted the Shaman. "Take six others with you," she advised, "and a large basket. You will find the Daughter of the Sun dancing with the ghosts in Tsusgina'i. Each of you must touch her with a sourwood rod. When she falls to the ground, put her into the basket and secure the lid. Then bring her back here."

"This we shall do," answered Dancing Drum. He chose six of the swiftest stickball players in the village.

They were about to leave for the Darkening-land when the Shaman cautioned, "Once you have her in the basket, do not lift the lid."

For days, the runners followed the path to the Land of the Spirits. At the end of the seventh day, they heard drums and chanting, and then they saw the ghosts, circling around a low fire. The Daughter of the Sun danced in the outer ring, heel-toe, heel-toe.

From their hiding place in the shrubs, Dancing Drum and his companions took turns reaching out with their sourwood rods. Each time the Daughter of the Sun passed, one of them touched her. Dancing Drum's rod was the seventh. As it brushed her, she collapsed. The ghosts seemed not to notice, so the boys hastily picked her up, put her into their basket, and secured the lid tightly.

After a time, the Daughter of the Sun started moving around in the basket. "Let me out!" she called to the runners. "I must eat!" At first, the seven ignored her. Then she called, "Let me out! I must have water!" Again her plea went unanswered.

When they were almost to the village, the basket started to shake. "Let me out," called the Daughter of the Sun. This time, her voice sounded strangled. "I cannot breathe!" she croaked. Dancing Drum was afraid she might die again, so he opened the lid a tiny crack.

Suddenly, a flapping sound came from inside the basket, and a flash of red flew past, followed by the "Kwish, kwish, kwish!" cry of a redbird. Not sure what had happened, Dancing Drum quickly refastened the lid and hurried with his companions back to the village.

Once there, the Shaman opened the basket. It was empty! The Daughter of the Sun had been transformed into the redbird. "You disobeyed," the Shaman said to Dancing Drum. "For this, souls can no longer be returned from the Land of the Spirits."

Dancing Drum hung his head, and Grandmother Sun, watching from the Sky World, began to weep. She cried so hard, her tears filled Long Man to overflowing, threatening a great flood over the land.

"What shall we do?" The People cried.

"We shall sing!" declared Dancing Drum. So The People put on their most beautiful clothes of embroidered buckskins. They wore necklaces of deer and panther teeth, and painted their faces white. They lifted their faces to the sky and chanted for Grandmother Sun. They drummed and kept rhythm with their gourd rattles. But still Grandmother Sun grieved.

Finally, Dancing Drum left the singing and went to his lodge for his own drum. It had been a special gift from his grandfather. He filled the hollow log with water and dampened the groundhog skin. At last he was ready. Returning to the group of singers, he sat and began playing his own song.

From the Land of the Sky People, Grandmother Sun heard the new music. She stopped crying and looked down to see her beautiful people smiling up at her. She saw them offering their special dances and she heard their special song.

Dancing Drum lifted his face to the sky as he played from his heart for his ancestors, for his people, and for his land. And as he played, Grandmother Sun came out of her house to once again smile down on her Children of the Mountain.

Knoxville, Tennessee

by Nikki Giovanni

I always like summer
best
you can eat fresh corn
from daddy's garden
and okra
and greens
and cabbage
and lots of
barbecue
and buttermilk
and homemade ice-cream
at the church picnic
and listen to
gospel music
outside
at the church
homecoming
and go to the mountains with
your grandmother
and go barefooted
and be warm
all the time
not only when you go to bed
and sleep

Anansi's Fishing Expedition

by Harold Courlander & George Herzog

There are many African stories about Anansi, the trickster. Sometimes Anansi appears as a spider, and other times, as here, he is a man. Always, Anansi tries to avoid work by tricking someone else into doing it for him. When Africans were brought to the Americas, they carried their folktales with them. Anansi became B'rer Rabbit, a well-known character in Southern storytelling.

In the country of Ashanti, not far from the edge of the great West African forest, there was a man named Anansi, who was known to all the people for miles around. Anansi was not a great hunter, or a great worker, or a great warrior. His specialty was being clever. He liked to outwit people. He liked to live well, and to have other people do things for him. But because all the people of the country knew about Anansi and had had trouble with him he had to keep thinking of new ways to get something for nothing.

One day Anansi was sitting in the village when a man named Osansa came along.

"I have an idea," Anansi said. "Why don't we go and set fish traps together? Then we shall sell the fish and be quite rich."

But Osansa knew Anansi's reputation very well, and so he said:

"No, I have as much food as I can eat or sell. I am rich enough. Why don't you set your fish traps by yourself?"

"Ha! Fish alone? Then I'd have to do all the work!" Anansi said. "What I need is a fool for a partner."

Osansa went away, and after a while another man named Anene came along.

"I have an idea," Anansi said. "Why don't the two of us go and set fish traps together? Then we shall sell the fish and be quite rich."

Anene knew Anansi very well too, but he seemed to listen thoughtfully.

"That sounds like a fine idea," he said. "Two people can catch more fish than one. Yes, I'll do it."

The news went rapidly around the village that Anansi and Anene were going on a fishing expedition together. Osansa met Anene in the market and said:

"We hear you are going to trap fish with Anansi. Don't you know he is trying to make a fool of you? He has told everyone that he needs a fool to go fishing with him. He wants someone to set the fish traps and do all the work, while he gets all the money for the fish."

"Don't worry, friend Osansa, I won't be Anansi's fool," Anene said.

Early the next morning Anansi and Anene went into the woods to cut palm branches to make their fish traps.

Anansi was busy thinking how he could make Anene do most of the work. But when they came to the place where the palm trees grew, Anene said to Anansi:

"Give me the knife, Anansi. I shall cut the branches for the traps. We are partners. We share everything. My part of the work will be to cut branches, your part of the work will be to get tired for me."

"Just a minute, let me think," Anansi said. "Why should I be the one to get tired?"

"Well, when there's work to be done someone must get tired," Anene said. "That's the way it is. So if I cut the branches the least you can do is to get tired for me."

"Hah, you take me for a fool?" Anansi said. "Give me the knife. I shall cut the branches and *you* get tired for *me!*"

So Anansi took the knife and began cutting the branches from the trees. Every time he chopped, Anene grunted. Anene sat down in the shade and groaned from weariness, while Anansi chopped and hacked and sweated. Finally the wood for the fish traps was cut. Anansi tied it up into a big bundle. Anene got up from the ground holding his back and moaning.

"Anansi, let me carry the bundle of wood now, and you can get tired for me," Anene said.

"Oh, no, my friend Anene," Anansi said, "I am not that simple minded. I'll carry the wood myself, and you can take the weariness for me."

So he hoisted the bundle to the top of his head and the two of them started back to the village. Anene groaned all the way.

"Oh, oh!" he moaned. "Take it easy, Anansi! Oh, oh!"

When they came to the village Anene said:

"Let me make the fish traps, Anansi, and you just sit down and get tired for me."

"Oh, no," Anansi said. "You just keep on as you are." And he made the fish traps while Anene lay on his back in the shade with his eyes closed, moaning and groaning.

And while he was making the traps, working in the heat with perspiration running down his face and chest, Anansi looked at Anene lying there taking all his weariness and sore muscles for him, and he shook his head and clucked his tongue.

"Anene thinks he is intelligent," he said to himself. "Yet look at him moaning and groaning there, practically dying from weariness!"

When the fish traps were done Anene climbed to his feet and said, "Anansi, my friend, now let me carry the fish traps to the water, and you can get tired for me."

"Oh, no," Anansi said. "You just come along and do your share. I'll do the carrying, you do the getting-tired."

So they went down to the water, Anansi carrying and Anene moaning. When they arrived, Anene said to Anansi:

"Now wait a minute, Anansi, we ought to think things over here. There are sharks in this water. Someone is apt to get hurt. So let me go in and set the traps, and should a shark bite me, then you can die for me."

"Wah!" Anansi howled. "Listen to that! What do you take me for? I'll go in the water and set the traps myself, and if I am bitten, then *you* can die for *me!*" So he took the fish traps out into the water and set them, and then the two of them went back to the village.

The next morning when they went down to inspect the traps they found just four fish. Anene spoke first.

"Anansi, there are only four fish here. You take them. Tomorrow there will probably be more, and then I'll take my turn."

"Now, what do you take me for?" Anansi said indignantly. "Do you think I am simple-minded? Oh, no, Anene, you take the four fish and I'll take my turn tomorrow."

So Anene took the four fish and carried them to town and sold them.

Next day when they came down to the fish traps, Anene said:

"Look, there are only eight fish here. I'm glad it's your turn, because tomorrow there doubtless will be more."

"Just a minute," Anansi said. "You want me to take today's fish so that tomorrow you get a bigger catch? Oh no, these are all yours, partner. Tomorrow I'll take my share."

So Anene took the eight fish and carried them to town and sold them.

Next day when they came to look in the traps they found 16 fish.

"Anansi," Anene said, "take the 16 fish. Little ones, too. I'll take my turn tomorrow."

"Of course you'll take your turn tomorrow, it's my turn today," Anansi said. He stopped to think. "Well now, you are trying to make a fool out of me again! You want me to take these 16 miserable little fish so that you can get the big catch tomorrow, don't you? Well, it's a good thing I'm alert! You take the 16 today and I'll take the big catch tomorrow!"

So Anene carried the 16 fish to the market and sold them.

Next day they came to the traps and took the fish out. But by this time the traps had rotted in the water.

"Well, it's certainly your turn today," Anene said. "And I'm very glad of that. Look, the fish traps are rotten and worn out. We can't use them any more. I'll tell you what—you take the fish to town and sell them, and I'll take the rotten fish traps and sell them. The fish traps will bring an excellent price. What a wonderful idea!"

"Hm," Anansi said. "Just a moment, don't be in such a hurry. I'll take the fish traps and sell them myself. If there's such a good price to be had, why shouldn't I get it instead of you? Oh, no, you take the fish, my friend."

Anansi hoisted the rotten fish traps up on his head and started off for town. Anene followed him, carrying the fish. When they arrived in the town Anene sold his fish in the market, while Anansi walked back and forth singing loudly:

"I am selling rotten fish traps! I am selling wonderful rotten fish traps!"

But no one wanted rotten fish traps, and the townspeople were angry that Anansi thought they were so stupid they would buy them. All day long Anansi wandered through the town singing:

"Get your rotten fish traps here! I am selling wonderful rotten fish traps!"

Finally the head man of the town heard about the affair. He too became very angry, and he sent messengers for Anansi. When they brought Anansi to him he asked indignantly:

"What do you think you are doing, anyway? What kind of

nonsense is this you are trying to put over the people of the town?"

"I'm selling rotten fish traps," Anansi said, "very excellent rotten fish traps."

"Now what do you take us for?" the chief of the town said. "Do you think we are ignorant people? Your friend Anene came and sold good fish, which the people want, but you come trying to sell something that isn't good for anything and just smell the town up with your rotten fish traps. It's an outrage. You insult us."

The head man turned to the townspeople who stood near by, listening.

"Take him away and whip him," he said.

The men took Anansi out to the town gate and beat him with sticks. Anansi shouted and yelled and made a great noise. When at last they turned him loose, Anene said to him:

"Anansi, this ought to be a lesson to you. You wanted a fool to go fishing with you, but you didn't have to look so hard to find one. You were a fool yourself."

Anansi nodded his head.

"Yes," he said thoughtfully, rubbing his back and his legs where they had beat him. And he looked reproachfully at Anene. "But what kind of partner are you? At least you could have taken the pain while I took the beating."

Birdfoot's Grandpa

by Joseph Bruchac

The old man
must have stopped our car
two dozen times to climb out
and gather into his hands
the small toads blinded
by our lights and leaping,
live drops of rain.

The rain was falling,
a mist about his white hair
and I kept saying
you can't save them all,
accept it, get back in
we've got places to go.

But, leathery hands full
of wet brown life,
knee deep in the summer
roadside grass,
he just smiled and said
they have places to go to
too.

Rachel Carson: Friend of the Earth

by Francene Sabin

Rachel Carson's book Silent Spring *transformed the way many people thought about ecology. It triggered the growth of the environmental movement, which helped protect Earth from further damage from dangerous chemicals. Carson's career is proof that one person can make a dramatic difference.*

Every spring, clouds of annoying mosquitoes appeared over the marshland, so a plane was sent up to spray a pesticide called DDT. The pesticide really worked—it killed almost all of the mosquitoes. This made people happy . . . for a short time.

Then birds and fish began to die. There were fewer butterflies that summer. Many birds' eggs didn't hatch. Bumblebees and grasshoppers began to disappear. All this happened because DDT was in the water, in the soil, on trees and shrubs and grasses.

The same thing was happening all around the world. Cows grazed on grass poisoned by pesticides, and traces of these chemicals were found in their milk. People drank milk and ate meat, vegetables, and fish—all carrying traces of pesticides.

129

Earth was being poisoned and nobody paid attention. Then, in 1962, a book appeared. It was called *Silent Spring*, by Rachel L. Carson. Like the rings made by a pebble dropped into a pool, the book's message spread. It showed us that our world is doomed if we continue to poison it with dangerous chemicals.

Today we know how fragile our Earth can be. Today we know the words *environment, ecology, endangered species, food chain,* and *balance of nature.* For this knowledge the world must thank Rachel Carson.

When she wrote *Silent Spring*, Carson felt that there was an important story to tell. She knew that people didn't have to be scientists to understand—they just needed to be told things in an honest and clear way. Honest and clear—those are the words that describe Rachel Carson's writing and thinking and the person she was.

Rachel Louise Carson was born on May 27, 1907, in Springdale, near Pittsburgh, Pennsylvania. Her parents, Maria and Robert Carson, already had two children: eight-year-old Robert, Jr. and 10-year-old Marian.

The Carsons' house was in the country. Mrs. Carson cooked the family's meals on a wood-burning stove. Like many homes in the early 1900s, the house had no gas or electricity and no running water. The Carsons used oil lamps or candles for lighting, and their only heat came from a fireplace in the parlor.

Rachel's family kept chickens, a cow, a few pigs, and some rabbits. They also grew their own vegetables. Like the early pioneers, the Carsons kept their food fresh in a springhouse. Rachel's father built a small enclosure of stone and wood over an ice-cold spring that bubbled up from the ground near the house. This natural refrigerator kept the food cold and also protected it from wild animals. And the frosty, clear water was delicious to drink.

The Carsons owned 65 acres of land, most of it woods. It was natural, unspoiled, and beautiful. Marian, Robert, and

Rachel loved to wander in the woodland world, observing all kinds of animals and birds. They ate apples from their orchard and fresh vegetables from their garden. The children fished in the sparkling brook that wound through the woods and picked wild raspberries and huckleberries, eating almost as many as they brought home for pies and jams.

The Carsons respected all the life on their land. Mrs. Carson didn't even like to kill insects. Whenever she found a spider or beetle in the house, she scooped it up and carried it outside. "Insects mean us no harm," Mrs. Carson told the children. "And we have no reason to harm them."

When Rachel was grown up, she remembered her mother's example. As a scientist, Rachel Carson often collected live specimens for study. But she did not throw them away when her work was done. Instead, she kept the fish, clams, crabs, and other creatures alive in a bucket of seawater. As soon as she could, she returned them to their natural habitat.

Mrs. Carson showed Rachel many things in the woods and fields around their house. They watched chipmunks dash around, collecting acorns for the winter. They saw golden butterflies landing lightly on wildflower blossoms and birds building nests and feeding their chirping babies.

"Close your eyes, Rachel," Mrs. Carson said. "Listen carefully." There was a symphony of sounds around them—singing birds, whirring insects, rustling leaves.

Maria McLean Carson loved to teach. She was never too busy to answer questions, to read aloud, or to go on a "discovery" walk through the woods. Mr. Carson's job with a power company often kept him away from home. Robert, Jr. and Marian were busy with school, friends, and hobbies. Mrs. Carson and Rachel were often left to themselves.

Mrs. Carson had once been a schoolteacher. She graduated from the Washington (Pennsylvania) Seminary in 1887, where she won special honors in Latin. She was also a talented musician who composed music and taught piano and singing.

But when Maria McLean married Robert Carson, she had to

stop teaching. In those days, female teachers were forced to leave their jobs if they got married. It was considered shameful for a wife to work outside her home. Many businesses refused to hire women at all.

An unmarried, educated woman could be a teacher, office assistant, or librarian. A married woman, educated or not, had no career choices. She was expected to stay home and keep house, and if she needed to earn money, she had to do it at home. But there were not many ways to do that.

Because the Carson family was always short of money, Rachel's mother earned a little by giving piano lessons in the parlor. But Mrs. Carson did not have many students, since their house was too far away for most children to come for lessons. Instead, she poured her talent and dreams into Rachel.

When Rachel started first grade, she was far ahead of the other children. She had the best grades in the class, but she also had the worst attendance record at Springdale Elementary School, because she was often sick with a cold or sore throat.

Whenever Rachel missed school she did all her homework, and more. If she asked her mother to explain something, Mrs. Carson always said, "That's an interesting question. Let's see if you can find the answer and explain it to me." Then Rachel looked through books, hunting for answers to "How?" and "Why?" That way Rachel learned to do research and to think things through.

Rachel also loved to write. She wrote her first "book" when she was in second grade. It was about animals, birds, fish, and bugs, with a drawing and a short poem on each page. Her drawings were quite good. They really looked like the mice, frogs, and other living things Rachel saw in the woods.

Rachel was very proud of her book and gave it to her father as a birthday present. Mr. Carson was full of praise for his daughter. "What a wonderful book!" he said. "You're a fine writer, Rachel. I'm so proud of you!"

Every month, Rachel read a children's magazine called *St. Nicholas*. It had stories, poems, puzzles, games, drawings, and a section for pieces written by young readers. The best of these contributions were awarded gold and silver badges.

When she was eight years old, Rachel began to send poems and stories to *St. Nicholas*. They were always returned with kind words. Then, in September, 1918, Rachel received a $10 check from the magazine for a story called "A Battle in the Clouds."

Rachel's story was about a World War I airplane battle. In 1918 the United States was at war with Germany, and Rachel's brother, Robert, was in the U.S. Army Aviation Service, training to be a pilot. One time, when he was home on leave, Robert told his family about a brave fellow airman. Rachel wrote the story in her own words and sent it to *St. Nicholas*. It won the silver badge.

Rachel kept writing and sending stories to *St. Nicholas*. Every day, on the way home from school, she opened the mailbox hopefully. Her efforts were rewarded in February, 1919, with a gold badge story, and then another in August of that same year. Now she had 30 dollars in the bank for her college fund. Best of all, there was her name—Rachel L. Carson—in the magazine!

Everyone said a writer had to learn about a lot of things. So Rachel made up her mind to do just that. In her high-school yearbook, her classmates wrote:

> Rachel's like the mid-day sun
> Always very bright
> Never stops studying
> 'Til she gets it right.

However, there was still time for fun. Rachel was on the field-hockey team at school and played the piano for family sing-alongs on weekends. And whenever she could, she wandered through the fields and woods.

In 1925, when she was 18, Rachel graduated from high school. She had very high grades and won a college scholarship to the Pennsylvania College for Women (PCW), in nearby Pittsburgh.

PCW was a small school, with just 300 students. Mrs.

Carson said, "It's perfect, Rachel dear. The classes will be small, and every student will get a lot of attention. And you'll be able to come home any time you want."

The college *was* ideal for young Rachel. She dived into her studies, and into her new life away from home. As a freshman, she took courses in math, music, history, French, and English. She also became a reporter for the school newspaper, *The Arrow*. Carson wanted to become a professional writer and practiced her writing every day.

In Carson's sophomore year, she had to take a course in biology. This class changed her whole life. Professor Mary Scott Skinker, her biology teacher, was tough. Skinker's students had to do a great deal of textbook reading and laboratory experiments. Nobody passed her class without studying hard, and nobody got an A without really earning it.

In those days, many people said that women weren't able to be real scientists. Professor Skinker didn't agree. She said, "Give women the same work, make the same demands, and they will do just as well as men." For Rachel Carson, that was more than true. She proved it by getting an A for the class. In addition, the biology course gave her a new goal. Although she still loved writing, she decided to become a biologist.

For the rest of her college years, Carson took many science courses and worked on her own projects. Carson's main interest was the animal life around her. She studied turtles, frogs, grasshoppers, crayfish, and other small local creatures. And, of course, she continued to write.

In May, 1929, Rachel Carson graduated from college with high honors. She was awarded a summer-study fellowship at the Marine Biological Laboratory in Woods Hole, Massachusetts. She was also given a one-year scholarship to Johns Hopkins University, in Baltimore, Maryland, where she planned to study for a master's degree in zoology. (Zoology is the branch of biology that deals with the animal kingdom and its members.)

Rachel Carson's first summer at Woods Hole was like finding a treasure. She had read about the ocean all her life, but she had never seen it. Now she had two whole months on Cape Cod, right at the edge of the Atlantic. Here she discovered sand dunes and beach grasses, gulls and sandpipers, crabs and clams, and the ocean itself, with its rolling surf and breakers crashing to the shore. For Carson, it was instant love. "Someday," she promised herself, "I will live close to the ocean."

By the end of the summer of 1929, Carson had no doubts about her future. She was going to be a marine biologist and study the life of the sea. But first it was on to Johns Hopkins to study for her master's degree.

Rachel Carson's graduate work was very hard. She spent many hours doing library research and she spent many more in the laboratory, bent over a microscope. There was no time for a social life or sports. Sometimes she was so busy, she even forgot to eat lunch.

When school had begun, in the fall of 1929, the Carsons sold their Pennsylvania home and moved to Baltimore. They bought a small house near the Johns Hopkins campus. At this time, the Great Depression was just beginning. Life was difficult throughout the world. In the United States, factories closed and millions of people were out of work. It was just as bad for farmers when a few years of no rain turned rich farms into dusty wastelands. Like many people, the Carsons had a tough time paying their bills.

Rachel Carson felt lucky to have her scholarship, which paid for her first year's schooling. When summer came, she worked as a teaching assistant in the university's summer school. The title "teaching assistant" sounded a lot more important than it was. Carson washed laboratory glassware, cleaned tables, and set up equipment for each class. But the job brought in money, and she welcomed it.

When Carson's scholarship ended, she still needed two more years of schooling to complete her degree. Those years meant one grinding day after another, because Carson needed to work while she attended school. One of her jobs was as a teaching assistant in biology at Johns Hopkins. For a second job, she was a lab assistant to one of her professors. And her third job was as a part-time assistant in the zoology department at the University of Maryland, which was a 35-mile bus trip each way. That took precious hours out of Carson's week, but she needed the money to pay for school. And she was determined not to give up.

Years later, a male classmate remembered Carson's tough schedule. "We used to feel sorry for Rachel," he said, "and we told her so. In those days, we didn't think a woman was up to being a scientist. And we certainly didn't think a woman could work two or three jobs, go to school, commute back and forth, get top grades—and survive."

Carson did more than survive. She earned excellent marks and received her master's degree in marine zoology in the spring of 1932. For the next three years, she struggled to earn a living at part-time jobs. Meanwhile, she kept applying for full-time scientific work. But museums, universities, and industries did not hire female scientists in those days. Things were not much easier for Rachel Carson in the 1930s than they had been for her mother 40 years earlier.

The Depression continued to affect the Carsons. Robert, Jr. lost his job and came to live with the family. So did Marian and her two children. Robert earned a little money repairing radios and had a small pension. But Rachel was the main support of the family.

When Mr. Carson died in July of 1935, his pension stopped. Now Rachel needed a full-time job. When the next U.S. Government Civil Service examination was given, Carson took it. She was the only woman applicant, and she received the highest test score. Soon after, she was hired by the Department of the Interior as a junior aquatic biologist in the Bureau of Fisheries. Her salary was $2,000 a year.

Carson's title was "biologist," but she didn't work in a laboratory or aboard a scientific research ship. She wrote radio scripts about fish and other marine life. These were part of a series called "Romance Under the Waters." Carson's talent shone through. The scripts were so good, the Bureau published them as a booklet. Carson also earned extra money writing articles for the *Baltimore Sun* newspaper and for magazines.

In September, 1937, the *Atlantic Monthly* Magazine published "Undersea," by Rachel Carson. It introduced the reader to the sights, sounds, tastes, and feelings of ocean creatures and asked the readers to imagine living under the sea. It was a very unusual article.

"Undersea" became the basis of *Under the Sea Wind,* Carson's first book. Reviewers everywhere praised the book, but it was published in November, 1941, one month before the United States entered World War II. People were not interested in reading a calm book about the ocean while the world was at war.

During World War II, the Bureau of Fisheries, now called the Fish and Wildlife Service, urged Americans to eat more fish. Rachel Carson's job was to write a series of booklets about freshwater and saltwater fish and shellfish. She described how they lived, how they were caught, and how to prepare and serve them.

The booklets were well-written and very useful. They were quoted frequently in magazines and newspapers and on radio programs. But Rachel Carson got no recognition for her fine work. All the credit went to the Fish and Wildlife Service.

After the war ended in 1945, Carson was named editor of a new series of 12 booklets called "Conservation in Action." She wrote several of the booklets herself. The series told about wildlife in the United States. Each booklet was full of colorful illustrations and fascinating facts about plants, animals, insects, and the land itself.

As she worked on "Conservation in Action," Carson began to worry about the environment. In her introduction to the series, she wrote: "Wild creatures, like men, must have a place to live. As civilization creates cities, builds highways, and drains marshes, it takes away, little by little, the land that is suitable for wildlife. And as their spaces for living dwindle, the wildlife populations themselves decline."

She also wrote, "For all the people, the preservation of wildlife and wildlife habitat means also the preservation of the basic resources of the earth, which men, as well as animals, must have in order to live. Wildlife, water, forests, grasslands— all are part of man's essential environment."

But at that time, even Carson did not realize how serious the problem was. In 1948 her greatest scientific interest and her greatest pleasure was the ocean. Since her first trip to Woods Hole, in 1929, she had one ambition. She wanted to write a book about the sea that would be scientific, interesting, and understood by everyone.

In 1949 Carson took a leave of absence from her job. She studied the Atlantic Ocean from a Fish and Wildlife survey ship. She went deep-sea diving off the Florida coast and she also examined many forms of sea life in the laboratory. Finally, in July of 1950, her book, *The Sea Around Us,* was finished.

Even before the book was published, it won science awards, and sections of it appeared in *The New Yorker* magazine. When *The Sea Around Us* went on sale in book-stores in 1951, it was a sensation. For more than a year and a half it was on *The New York Times* best-seller list. Many magazines reprinted chapters and condensed parts of the book. It was translated into many languages and quoted around the world.

Rachel Carson was famous. When *Under the Sea Wind* was reissued, it also became a best seller. Hollywood made a documentary film of *The Sea Around Us,* which won an Academy Award. After years of struggling, Carson quit her job to write full-time. And she was able to afford another dream: she bought land on the coast of Maine and had a cottage built, facing the sea.

There Carson worked on her next book, *The Edge of the Sea.* It was all about the shoreline: the plants and animals, the insects, the shifting sands. Carson was especially interested in tide pools, the protected pockets of shallow water where many sea creatures live.

Bob Hines, Carson's illustrator at the Fish and Wildlife Service, spent many days at the tide pools with her. Carson wanted the book's drawings to make all the creatures look alive and natural. Hines's fine drawings did that and they helped to make *The Edge of the Sea* a huge success when it came out in 1955.

The next few years brought many changes to Carson's life. Her niece, Marjorie, died, and Rachel adopted her five-year-old son, Roger. Not long after that, her mother died. It was a sad time, but her writing and Roger kept Carson busy. He was a bright little boy and raising him made Rachel Carson very happy. She wanted his life to be wonderful, and she began to worry about the world of the future—his world.

Carson wanted to write a short article about the dangers of pesticides. She started to do research and was horrified by what she learned. Because the story was too big to tell in an article, Carson decided to write a book. As a scientist, she wanted it to be accurate. As a writer, she wanted her words to be clear. As a human being who cared about the future and all the children like Roger, she wanted people to pay attention.

Rachel Carson was a very private person who didn't like to call attention to herself. She didn't find it easy to write harsh words about industries and governments. But now she had to speak out, even if it made people angry and shattered the privacy she treasured.

When *Silent Spring* was published in 1962, it rocked the world like a giant earthquake. Rachel Carson's words were clear and simple. She described what happens when a chemical pesticide like DDT is used. She told about the effects of pesticides on fish and wildlife, on farms, on the food we eat, and on our health.

Reactions to the book were strong and immediate. Articles appeared, attacking her as a kook, a hysterical woman, a fanatic opposed to progress, and a non-scientist. Other articles praised her courage for speaking out. But the most important result was that people *did* begin to pay attention to the dangers Carson wrote about.

President John F. Kennedy appointed a committee to study pesticides. Rachel Carson met with the committee and testified before the United States Congress. Secretary of the Interior Stewart L. Udall said, "Rachel Carson alerted us to the subtle dangers of an Age of Poisons. She made us realize that we had allowed our fascination with chemicals to override our wisdom in their use."

Colleges and universities gave Rachel Carson honorary degrees. She was elected to the American Academy of Arts and Sciences, and honored by scientific groups and government agencies. Much of her time was spent making speeches, alerting the world to the threats against the environment.

Carson looked tired and pale during these busy months. Some people thought her heavy schedule was the reason, but her close friends knew the truth. Carson had been suffering from cancer since the spring of 1960. Surgery and radiation treatments helped a little, but not enough. She grew weaker and suffered a heart attack in 1963. Knowing the end was near, she retired to her beach cottage in Maine. There, close to the sea she loved so deeply, Rachel Carson died on April 14, 1964.

After her death, a *New York Times* editor wrote: "She was a biologist, not a crusader, but the power of her knowledge and the beauty of her language combined to make Rachel Carson one of the most influential women of our time."

The Attack

by Joseph Gallagher

*If alien beings wanted to destroy Earth, how would
they go about it? The author was a high-school student
in Massachusetts when he wrote this story.*

As the captain looked down, he saw the planet he was
going to destroy: Earth. He had several brilliant plans in
mind as to how to destroy this planet.

"First Mate Nako!" yelled the captain. Soon the first mate of
the starship stood beside him.

"Yes, Captain?"

"Do you know what I'm going to do to that planet below?"

"What, Captain?"

The captain grinned and said, "I will contaminate their
water supply! I'll put tons of filth in it! The sea life will die off
slowly, and soon their food chain will crumble. I—"

"Excuse me, Captain, but aren't they doing that already?"

The captain frowned and said, "What?"

"Yes, Captain. Their water is already disgusting. The land life can't even drink it in some places. They pour tons of garbage into it every day, and the sea life is already dying off. Sorry."

After a pause, the captain said, "Well, never mind, never mind. Instead, I'll destroy the invisible wall that protects them from the sun's radiation! They will all become sick, and slowly—"

"They're doing that too, sir."

"—die off! Yes, a gruesome fate in—"The captain stopped, and looked at the first mate. "What did you say?"

"They're doing it. They have been producing materials that can slowly make holes in what they call the 'ozone layer.' It gives them a deadly skin disease."

"Hmmmm . . . then . . . I'll have our spies circulate a substance that will seem to make humans happy, but will actually kill them slowly. It will be highly addictive, and soon humans will do anything for more! Then we'll move in and—"

"It's already been done, sir. A lot of humans are already addicted to many such substances, and a few humans are making a real profit off them."

"Well, for Gnob's sake, Nako!" burst out the captain. "Why are they so bent on suicide?

"Oh, a few are trying to stop the planet's course of destruction, sir. It's just that hardly anyone listens to them."

The captain looked depressed. "Well, they've got us this time, Nako. I've run out of ideas." Suddenly a gleam came into the captain's eyes. "But wait! I have it! Listen to this, Nako! I shall LEAVE THEM ALONE!! That's it! In 1,000 years they'll have died off. What do you think of that, eh?"

"Fiendishly clever, sir," said Nako, stifling a yawn.

"Give the order to turn the ship, Nako," said the captain, chuckling. The first mate gave the order, and the huge starship turned toward home.

Last Summer

by Tricia Springstubb

The time comes when you must move on, but what if you're not ready? Do you hang back while your best friend rushes forward? Can you take the chance of being left behind?

On the last day of sixth grade Eunice Gottlieb stared out the window of her classroom. It was a hot, blue, glorious day, which made the fact that she felt absolutely terrible all the more ridiculous. This was a day you were supposed to look forward to! Onward, upward, et cetera! If only the windows of her classroom didn't give directly onto the front lawn of the junior high. If only for weeks and weeks now she hadn't had to watch those seventh, eighth, and ninth graders going in and out. Speak of the devil—here they come now. When the last bell rang over there they flew out as if propelled by some inner explosion, and you could tell that if a measly sixth grader got in their way it would be just too bad for her. Junior-high girls wore makeup and somehow made their hair fluffy. They settled themselves into tight, impenetrable little groups, and they checked each other out. From head to foot. Inside out. Eunice saw the girls who had to walk home alone hurrying along with their heads down, trying to get out of sight as quickly as possible.

Oh God.

Holding an already ravaged pencil, she began to chew on it furiously. Her big sister, Millie, liked to tell her this habit caused lead poisoning, and that was why Eunice was so feebleminded. To think that Eunice had once considered Millie her life's greatest affliction. Little had she known what real trouble was.

Eunice's best friend, Joy McKenzie, came and stood beside her. They were supposed to be cleaning out their desks, but Joy's was, of course, already immaculate. Observing Eunice's weak-kneed state, she said, "Come on, don't tell me you're worrying again."

"All right. I won't tell you."

"What are you afraid of? They're just kids!"

"You know that's not true."

Joy squinted out the window. "Two legs, two arms, backpacks, and mouths full of gum—they're certainly not hippopotami."

Eunice waved her pencil, ignoring Joy's look of disgust at it. "We hardly know any of them! Next year we'll be in classes with kids we've never laid eyes on before. Sixty-six point six percent of the school will be older than us! On a scale of zero to ten, we'll be minus 15! Joy, we'll be the youngest, plus—" she gulped—"we'll be among absolute strangers!"

"Egad! I keep telling you, that's what's so great about it!" Joy tossed her long, gleaming, butterscotch-colored hair. "Junior high is a fresh start. This dumb class of ours—we've been together since kindergarten. We know each other backwards and forwards." She lowered her voice, and Mrs. Schwark raised an eyebrow. "Everyone knows Priscilla Berger is world champion blabbermouth, Mona Mahoney is afraid of her own shadow, Reggie Ackeroyd is a spoiled brat, you and I would swallow boiling oil for each other. . . . Admit it! Things have gotten positively incestuous."

That was one of those words Eunice couldn't have pronounced without a choking spasm and that Joy could drop with aplomb. It was true: Joy was no cowerer. She was quite capable of viewing junior high as an adventure, and over the past few weeks had tried to convince Eunice to feel the same way. Eunice, however, couldn't help looking out at those seventh, eighth, and ninth graders the way someone in a leaky boat would regard a river full of piranhas. When they smiled all she saw was teeth.

"But Joy, there's something nice about knowing where you stand. I mean—how do we know we'll fit in?"

"Fit in? What are we, puzzle pieces? We're individuals! Now stop chewing that pencil and come on away from this window—I'm starting to melt. Egad." She took a horrified sniff at her armpit. "I'm actually sweating."

Joy had been wearing antiperspirant for some time now. She'd had no trouble convincing her mother to let her, whereas Mrs. Gottlieb had laughed and told Eunice not to be silly. There was positively no chance that next year some eighth or ninth grader would sneak up behind Joy and announce "Beeeee-ohhhhh!" loudly enough to make the entire hallway lapse into mass hysterics. It occurred to Eunice that as long as she stayed best friends with Joy, she really had little to fear. And since their friendship was as unquestionable a force as gravity. . . . Just think of all they'd been through together! Losing their front teeth, getting chicken pox, joining Girl Scouts, quitting Girl Scouts, Joy's dance recitals (Eunice in the front row every time), Eunice's threats to disown her family (Joy never teasing when she relented), hitchhiking to Akron to see the Rolling Stones, getting punished for hitchhiking to Akron to see the Rolling Stones—if Eunice were to make a list entitled Memorable Events of My Life, Joy would have been present at every one.

Across the room Reggie Ackeroyd, skinny as a dragonfly, was complaining to Mrs. Schwark that she was going to have to spend the next two weeks with her father, and he was taking her to France.

"I want to go to Disney World. I've already been to Europe *twice*," she whined, "and it's *yucky*."

Priscilla Berger was blabbing on and on as usual, and as usual no one but mousy little Mona Mahoney was paying the slightest attention. Looking around the room Eunice decided that Joy was probably right: the air had grown decidedly stale. It was, after all, time for a change. As her father said about aging: I prefer it to the alternative.

Eunice gathered herself up. She tossed out all her mutilated pencils and handed in the rest of her books. She bid Mrs. Schwark goodbye and, with Joy, as ever, at her side, marched out the door. I am, she told herself, prepared to begin a new life.

For the first week or two of vacation Joy and Eunice followed their usual routine, getting together in the early afternoon, after Joy's dance or tennis or cello lesson, and deciding what to do. They rode no-handed down Cedar Hill; they lounged in the air-conditioned library reading magazines; they lay under Eunice's plum tree drinking pop and talking. They each got a second hole pierced in their left ears. Once or twice a week they went to the town pool. Eunice had never much liked going there—she preferred the lake—and this year especially she disliked it. The pool was a prime junior-high hangout and Eunice, though assuring herself she was ready for seventh grade, was definitely not ready to be observed in a bathing suit. Up until recently she'd had a more or less friendly feeling toward her body—it got her where she wanted to go and only rarely needed repairs—but now she saw that it was convex and concave in all the wrong places, and showed no signs of changing. Totally inadequate. That was what those junior-high kids with their piercing scalpel-eyes could do: make you feel your own body was a traitor. When they went to the pool Eunice kept her T-shirt on as long as possible. She jumped in the water only when baking on the concrete became unbearable, and as soon as she got out she pulled her shirt back on. Joy, on the other hand, spent all her time on the high dive. She loved diving almost as much as she did dancing. "I guess I just enjoy defying gravity," she sighed.

One afternoon as Eunice huddled in her T-shirt, pretending to do a crossword puzzle but really eyeing the junior-high crowd that had commandeered one whole half of the poolside, she saw a boy detach himself from the crowd and come sit by the ladder across from the diving board. He was tall, with dark eyes and careless, tangled hair and the kind of honeyish tan that some blonds get. Joy was climbing up the high dive, and Eunice thought idly that the boy looked like one of those that hovered in the background of Cover Girl ads—so handsome you just knew he couldn't have an original thought in his head.

Up on the high dive Joy paused, surveying the earthbound world. She gave a small, expert bounce and came sailing down, slipping into the water with just the faintest whisper of a whoosh. Though Eunice had viewed this performance dozens of times, she still felt like applauding. In another era, Eunice knew, Joy would have been called A Paragon of Grace.

Joy surfaced and shook her head, sending diamond-bright drops of water flying. She was across the pool in three strokes, swinging herself up the ladder—and stumbling. Joy never stumbled. But then she'd never had a boy with eyes like that staring up into her face, either.

Eunice watched Joy walk back around and dive again. The boy sat very still, but somehow like a coiled-up spring. As Joy swam across and climbed the ladder he didn't take his eyes off her. Eunice felt a shiver up her spine, though her unde-odoranted armpits were dripping.

Joy climbed the high dive once more, gave that small, businesslike bounce, and then—how did she do it? This time she seemed to drift down through the air in slow motion, as if she were an instant replay on Wide World of Sports or a magnolia petal blown loose in the breeze. There was only the barest ripple where she disappeared into the sky-blue water.

Eunice began to chew on her pencil.

This time when Joy climbed out she came straight to Eunice. Over her shoulder Eunice could see the boy turn to watch them. His eyes were like black stars.

In a voice uncharacteristically out of breath, Joy said, "That's enough."

But the next day she was at Eunice's early, already in her swimsuit.

"We went to the pool yesterday," said Eunice uneasily.

"It's too hot to do anything else."

"I thought we could go to the matinee at World East. It'll be arctic in there."

"Egad, Eu, stop whining. You sound like Reggie Ackeroyd. Air-conditioning is unhealthy. Let's go."

Eunice had to pedal hard to keep up with Joy, and by the time they reached the pool she was one big bucket of sweat. Hugging her armpits to her sides, she followed Joy out of the locker room—and saw the boy, sitting with a group of boys and girls, get up at once and come to sit by the ladder.

Eunice took a quick dip and then spread her towel next to Joy's, dropped in a hurried heap. One of the boy's friends yelled something to him and he turned his head just long enough to call something back. The friend pretended to fall down laughing.

"What a show-off!" screeched someone in Eunice's ear, just as Joy dove. It was Reggie Ackeroyd, yanking on the ridiculous marmalade-colored ponytail that spouted from the top of her bony head. "Does she think she's the only one in the world who can dive like that?"

Joy climbed out of the water and Eunice realized she was holding her breath, waiting for the boy to do something.

"I had private diving lessons last year." Reggie, who was one of the most emaciated people Eunice had ever seen, pulled on her ponytail. "But you won't catch me showing off like that! Want to see my waterproof watch? It's from Paris."

For the first time Joy looked at the boy.

Reggie crouched down next to Eunice, prepared to spread her towel, but Eunice shot her the kind of look that if looks could kill, would have put Reggie in the ambulance at once.

"Who does she think she is, anyway?" said Reggie feebly, and backed away.

Joy had a baby-sitting job for the next three afternoons, and Eunice didn't see her. She mooned around the house, causing her mother to ask if she felt all right.

"She looks lovesick to me," said Millie.

Eunice, staring out the window at the plum tree, did not deign to reply.

"The first time I fell in love was the summer after sixth grade," said Millie coming to stand beside her. "Paul Rinaldo. He had eyes like plums dipped in water, I swear. People who call it puppy love—they're either pathetic dullards or just don't remember. I'd have mugged my best friend if it would've made Paul Rinaldo like me, I swear."

"Spare me," said Eunice, but Millie wasn't listening. She stared out the window, her face rapt.

"Four years later and I still sometimes think of him. His father got transferred to New Mexico. I cried myself to sleep for a month, I swear."

"Bring on the violins."

Eunice ran up to her room. She pulled out a scrapbook she'd been saving and began pasting in mementos of things she and Joy had done together. Right on the front page she pasted the ancient photo of the two of them with their arms thrown around each other's shoulders, grinning without any front teeth.

She was working on it early the next afternoon when a pebble pinged off her screen. Looking down, she saw Joy on her 10-speed, a towel around her neck.

"You're here already? I didn't even eat lunch yet."

Joy dismissed this remark with a wave of her hand. "It's too hot to eat."

Lack of appetite—wasn't that one of those sure signs of love? Eunice, feeling a little queasy herself, held the scrapbook up to the window.

"I have something to show you!"

"Later, Eu! Come on!"

Eunice, with a growing sense of dread, went down. Joy was wearing a new wispy white blouse over a new hot-pink suit. As Eunice stared she blushed and gave a nervous laugh.

"It's my reward for spending three days taking care of those Musselman brats," she said, and then asked, "Do you think it looks okay?"

Seeing Joy self-conscious made Eunice feel very eerie. But not nearly as eerie as realizing that Joy had breasts. Breasts! Had she grown them in three days? Or had they been there for a while now, just not so noticeable in her old bleached-out suit?

"It looks . . . you know it looks great, Joy."

Joy's anxious expression vanished. "It's the first time I've gone shopping without you in a million years. I needed the Eunice Gottlieb Seal of Approval!"

As they rode to the pool Eunice told herself it was ridiculous to feel betrayed by two strategically placed bulges. Gliding no-handed down Cedar Hill, she tried to remember the time when she and Joy had bragged about how many days it had been since they'd had a bath. But it was like trying to recall how they'd ever been so disgusting as to wad up their cupcake papers and chew them. One look at Joy in her new suit and she knew those days were gone forever.

At the pool they showed their passes and went into the locker room, which smelled as usual like wet paper towels and hundred-year-old tennis shoes. Stepping across the cement floor which was pocked with grimy puddles, Eunice said loudly, "God. This place is so revolting."

"Huh? What are you so grumpy about?" Joy had already slipped out of her shorts and blouse and tossed them into the locker they shared.

"I'm not grumpy. I just wonder sometimes if swimming

here is worth the risk of contracting typhoid fever. Or," she added, making her voice meaningful, "worse."

She knew Joy knew what she meant. But Joy only made her don't-be-a-nerd grimace and, using the open locker door as a barre, began to do a series of dance warm-ups.

"I never liked coming here," Eunice went on, tugging off her own clothes, "even when we were little. Hey, remember swimming lessons? The only good part was free swim. We'd always be 'buddies.' Remember the time . . . ."

Joy nodded impatiently and glanced toward the door. Eunice, her heart sinking, tried one more tactic to delay their going out to the pool.

"I have to go to the bathroom," she said.

"Okay," said Joy, slinging her dazzlingly white towel around her neck. "Meet you outside." And away she danced.

Eunice sat down on the bench. Her own towel slipped into a puddle, and she watched one corner soak up athlete's foot. She could just put her clothes on and ride home. Imagine Joy's surprise when she found her best friend gone! Found herself *alone.* Joy could talk all she wanted about how she didn't care about "fitting in," but when it came right down to it even she would have to admit there was nothing scarier or lonelier than being the odd one out. Joy could be thoughtless, but as her best friend, Eunice owed it to her not to abandon her.

Eunice picked up her pencil and crossword book. Clutching her disease-ridden towel to her nonexistent chest, she marched out the door just in time to see the dark-eyed, tangle-haired boy speak to Joy for the first time. Joy froze, there on the ladder, like someone in a fairy tale tapped by a magic wand. And then, as Eunice watched, Joy answered him.

Did a cloud really pass across the sun?

"I don't know why I bother to come to this yucky pool at all," whined Reggie Ackeroyd in Eunice's ear. "Considering I have my own Olympic-sized pool in my own backyard."

The boy stood up, and he and Joy walked over to a bench together. His friends yelled something, but he ignored them.

Joy bent her head and regarded one slender, extended foot as the boy sat down. Looking up into Joy's face, he went on talking to her.

Eunice stumbled, collapsing onto her towel.

"It's kidney-shaped," said Reggie, and sat right down beside her.

That was how it went. Nearly every afternoon Joy would call for Eunice, they would ride to the pool together, and the boy would claim her. His name was Robert Moffett and he was going to be in eighth grade. He lived on the other side of Fairmount, he played soccer, and last year he had been vice president of his class. Joy related all this to Eunice exactly as she had every detail of her life: as if Eunice had a right to know and as if, of course, Eunice would be interested.

"He likes me," she said, staring up into the plum tree, where the fruit was plump and ripening. "The first time he saw me there on the diving board, he decided he wanted to get to know me."

Eunice swallowed. "You mean he . . . he actually came right out and told you that?"

Joy laughed in a way Eunice had never heard before. "Uh huh. You could tell it never entered his cement head that I might not like him back. Not *Robert Moffett*." She laughed again.

Eunice felt a flicker of hope. Pulling a leaf off the tree she said, "He's so handsome. I mean, it's almost unnatural." She studied Joy's upturned face, but Joy only gave that laugh again. Flirty, that's what it is, Eunice realized with horror. She rushed on, "The first time I saw him I thought, 'Anyone that hand-some can't be capable of scratching his head and crossing the street at the same time.' And now you tell me he's not only dumb but conceited, too. What a shame."

Joy blinked, and turned to look at Eunice as if through a fog. "I didn't say that."

"Yes, you did."

"No, I didn't. I said . . . oh, I can't remember what I said."

She stood up slowly, yawning. "Lately I feel so . . . so sleepy!"
She laughed one more time and climbed onto her bike. Eunice
watched her go wobbling down the driveway as if, indeed, in a
trance.

Joy began wearing mascara—waterproof, of course. Once
they got to the pool she did one token dive, and then sat with
Robert Moffett and his cohort. For a few days Eunice, at Joy's
urging, sat with them too. Nobody talked to her, but nobody
made fun of her, either. She could see that Robert Moffett was
too big a big shot for anyone to bother his girlfriend's friend.

Then one day some of them began teasing a short
redheaded boy whose voice, they said, was exactly like Woody
Woodpecker's. This boy jumped up and rat-tailed his towel at
Robert Moffett. Robert and another boy grabbed his arms and
legs and started hauling him toward the pool. The girls
shrieked; the lifeguard blew her whistle; they dropped the boy
in an ignominious heap. Joy smiled and Eunice, watching
Woody Woodpecker attempt to pick himself up with dignity,
thought she would burst into tears.

The next day she told Joy she guessed she'd rather sit
alone.

"Why?"

"I don't fit in."

"Come on, Eu! You don't even try! You never say a word!"

"They're too smooth for me."

"You don't even know them! You're just judging them on
the surface!"

"Of course I am!" exploded Eunice. "That's how they judge
everyone else! Why shouldn't I judge them the same way?"

Joy turned the key in the locker she and Eunice shared
every day. "You don't know them," she said again, quietly.

"I don't want to."

"Okay." She handed Eunice the key. "It's up to you."

Still, day after day, Eunice went to the pool and lay doing
her crossword puzzles. She wasn't sure why, when Joy came

pinging a pebble on her screen every afternoon, she didn't just dump a bucket of water down on her head. Sometimes she told herself it was so that when Joy finally woke up and realized what creeps Robert and his gang were, she could turn and find her steadfast old friend waiting. Other times, usually late at night as she lay awake thinking of junior high (the Back-to-School ads had started, giving her acute heebie-jeebies), she thought it was to fool herself into feeling she and Joy still had some connection. As long as she was there baking in plain view on the concrete, Joy couldn't forget her completely.

"A three-letter word for 'vital juice,'" she said aloud.

"Sap," said Reggie Ackeroyd in her mosquito voice.

Reggie's paper-white skin was peeling from her nose to her toes. She wore a two-piece bright orange suit that even someone with Eunice's limited fashion sense could tell was a grievous mistake. But Reggie wasn't as dumb as she appeared. Between the two of them—Eunice chewing on her pencil, Reggie yanking on her ponytail—they solved puzzle after puzzle.

"Someday maybe you can come swim in my pool," Reggie said. "You should see it. It's beautiful. Everybody who sees it says it's the most beautiful pool they've ever seen."

She looked at Eunice with an eagerness that made Eunice wince.

And then one afternoon, when Eunice was expecting Joy to show up any minute, the phone rang.

"Eu? I'm not going swimming today."

"Oh?" Eunice, standing in the kitchen, gripped the edge of the sink. Joy and Robert had had a fight. It was over. There were still two weeks before school started, plenty of time to make up, become best friends again, and behave as if Robert Moffett had been the purest figment of the imagination . . . . "You're not?"

"No. Robert . . . Robert's taking me to the movies."

"Oh." Eunice focused on a bloated tea bag lying in the sink drain. "The movies."

"Yeah. We're going to see *Call of the Wild* at World East. It's supposed to be excellent." Joy paused. "Eu? Are you there?"

Eunice stared at the discarded tea bag. "World East? Better bring a sweater. The air-conditioning's arctic in there." She swallowed. "Unhealthy."

She could hear Joy draw a breath. She could see Joy's amber-colored eyebrows rush together the way they did before she began to speak carefully. Realizing how well she knew her friend made her eyes burn, and she gripped the sink all the harder.

"Eu, you're making too big a deal out of this. Just because we're going to the movies . . . ."

"I just don't want you to catch cold," Eunice interrupted, and even as she tried to stop herself something made her blunder on. "Of course you probably won't need a sweater after all. Just being with the mighty Robert Moffett will probably keep you plenty warm."

There was a silence in which Eunice, the blood pounding in her ears, didn't even try to imagine what Joy looked like.

"I'm sorry you're taking this this way," said Joy.

"What way?"

"Really sorry." And Joy hung up.

Eunice banged the receiver back in its cradle. She was already in her swimming suit, and without giving herself time to think she jumped on her bike and rode to the pool. As soon as she spread her towel, Reggie Ackeroyd materialized.

"You came by yourself," she said.

"You're so observant, Reggie. Have you ever considered a career as a private eye?" Eunice, to her horror, felt the back of her throat close up and her eyes fill with tears. She turned away. Wouldn't that just top it all off? To have a jerk like Reggie see her cry?

Reggie was quiet for a moment, then said, for the 17,000th time, "I don't know why I come to this yucky pool."

"Neither do I!" Eunice burst out, turning on her. "Neither do I! Why don't you just stay home and swim in your own

155

pool, if it's so great?"

Reggie tugged on her ponytail so hard Eunice could see her temples turn pink. She would, just then, have gladly yanked the fool thing clean off Reggie's head.

"You don't have to take it out on me," said Reggie, her lower lip trembling. "Just because your best friend dumped you . . . ."

"Are you totally crazy or what? Have you completely lost your marbles? Huh? Have you?"

"I know. I saw." Reggie was trying to gather up her stuff, fumbling and dropping everything. She picked up the cross-word book by mistake, and Eunice snatched it back.

We're not pieces of a puzzle, Joy had said, light-years ago. *We're individuals.* What a liar! She'd snatched the first chance she got to fit in, and Eunice could just go rot.

"I don't blame you for being jealous," snuffled Reggie, folding up her designer towel. "I'd be jealous, too. But you don't have to . . . ."

"Look, Reggie, let me give you some advice. There are times when you should just keep your mouth shut, understand?"

Reggie looked at her with pink eyes and red eyelids. "Want to come swim in my pool?"

Losers. It really did take one to know one.

"Sure. Fine. I'll come swim in your famous pool. What do I care?"

I t was a long ride back to Reggie's house, one of the Tudor-style near-mansions on Fairmount Boulevard. With every push of her pedals Eunice pushed back her thoughts. She couldn't stand to think of what she and Joy had said to each other. At Reggie's they dropped their bikes on the spectacularly green grass and walked around to the back. Lying there still and empty, reflecting the sky and the late summer flowers that surrounded it, the pool was as beautiful as Reggie had claimed.

"Go on," said Reggie happily. "Go on in. It's not cold."

Eunice sat on the pool's edge and dangled her feet in the

water. It was so quiet here—no shouting and splashing. She could actually hear a bird singing. The water smelled like water, not chemicals. Why, after all, did Reggie go to the foul town pool when she could have all this to herself?

Because no one wants to be alone. And Eunice felt the pain that had been building up come breaking over her.

Just then there was a familiar sound, and Eunice looked up to see Reggie bouncing on the end of the board. God! What was wrong with that girl? All knees and elbows—she'd no doubt do a bellywhopper, incur a concussion . . . .

But Reggie, with one more bounce, rose, cut down through the air like a sharp little knife, and sliced into the water.

For one moment she had been nearly as graceful as Joy.

She surfaced and, treading water, smiled shyly at Eunice.

"I didn't know you could dive like that."

"I told you I had private lessons."

"I know, but you never dive at the town pool."

"Yeah. I can't do it there. Only here, in my own pool." She hoisted herself out of the water and threw herself face down on a chaise lounge.

Eunice looked down into the water and saw her own ripply reflection. It was just how she felt—watery, wavery, all her edges gone liquid.

She let herself think of Joy, who right this very moment might be having her shoulder encircled by the stupid honey-tan arm of Robert Moffett. Just the way Eunice had encircled it, in that photo where they were both front-toothless. There was no escaping the fact: no matter what turned out with Robert Moffett, things would never be the same between her and Joy again. Joy, never a cowerer, had broken the old bond. She'd meant it when she said she was sorry—Eunice knew her well enough to know she'd truly meant it. But she'd done it anyway. She wanted to be friends with Eunice, but she wanted Robert too.

A little breeze wrinkled her reflection again, and a small yellow leaf came sailing by. Autumn. Seventh grade. So this was how it was. Inside everyone was a part that yearned to be liked and to fit in, and a part that was whole all by itself.

It was going to be a rough year.

"Do you want some lemonade?" shrilled Reggie. "Or a Coke?"

Eunice knew—she'd heard in that voice she knew so well—that Joy still wanted to be friends. Now it was up to Eunice.

"Or Seven-Up?" begged Reggie.

Eunice turned to look at her. "You really can dive," she said. Reggie's face swallowed itself up with delight at the first kind words Eunice had ever spoken to her.

"Or how about ice cream sodas? We have a machine that makes seltzer water. It's from France. We can have whatever we want, you know."

"Oh yeah?"

Eunice turned back to the pool. She looked down into the water, and saw her reflection slowly smooth itself out and stare back up at her.

(Acknowledgments continued from page 2)

"Since Hanna Moved Away" reprinted with the permission of Atheneum Books for Young Readers, an imprint of Simon & Schuster from *If I Were in Charge of the World and Other Worries* by Judith Viorst. Text copyright © 1981 Judith Viorst.

"A Nice Old-Fashioned Romance with Love Lyrics and Everything" from *My Name Is Aram,* copyright 1940 and renewed 1968 by William Saroyan, reprinted by permission of Harcourt Brace & Company.

Gift of the Nile. Copyright © 1993 Troll Associates.

"On the Vanity of Earthly Greatness" from *Gaily the Troubadour.* Copyright © 1936, Arthur Guiterman. Reprinted by permission of Louise H. Sclove.

"A Mother in Mannville" reprinted with the permission of Scribner, a Division of Simon & Schuster from *When the Whippoorwill* by Marjorie Kinnan Rawlings. Copyright © 1936, 1940 by Marjorie Kinnan Rawlings. Renewed 1964, 1968 by Norton Baskin.

"The Day the Batboy Played" reprinted with the permission of Simon & Schuster Books for Young Readers from *The Greatest Sports Stories Never Told* by Bruce Nash and Allan Zullo. Copyright © 1993 Nash & Zullo Productions, Inc.

"The Nauga Hunters" first appeared in *Merlyn's Pen: The National Magazines of Student Writing.* Reprinted by permission of Merlyn's Pen, East Greenwich, RI.

"Superman: The Neglected Parents" from *The Unsung Heroes* by Nathan Aaseng. Copyright 1989 by Lerner Publications Company. Used by permission of the publisher. All rights reserved.

"The One Who Watches" from *An Island Like You* by Judith Ortiz Cofer. Copyright © 1995 by Judith Ortiz Cofer. Reprinted by permission of the publisher, Orchard Books, New York.

Harriet Tubman: The Road to Freedom. Copyright © 1982 Troll Associates.

"Lineage" from *This Is My Century: New and Collected Poems* by Margaret Walker. Reprinted by permission of The University of Georgia Press.

"A Special Gift" © 1989 by Miriam Rinn. Originally appeared as "Marci's Chanukah Secret" in *Jewish Standard.* Reprinted by permission of the author.

"Father" by Gary Soto is from *Living Up the Street* (Dell, 1992). Used by permission of the author.

"Do Not Go Gentle Into That Good Night" by Dylan Thomas, from *The Poems of Dylan Thomas.* Copyright © 1952 by Dylan Thomas. Reprinted by permission of New Directions Publishing Corp. and J. M. Dent.

"Shark Bait" from *Dave Barry Is Not Making This Up* by Dave Barry. Copyright © 1994 by Dave Barry. Reprinted by permission of Crown Publishers, Inc.